HEALTHY
Vegan
Air Fryer
COOKBOOK

HEALTHY
Vegan
Air Fryer
COOKBOOK

Dana Angelo White, MS, RD, ATC

Publisher Mike Sanders
Editor Christopher Stolle
Art Director William Thomas
Compositor Ayanna Lacey
Photographer Kelley Jordan Schuyler
Proofreaders Georgette Beatty & Chrissy Guthrie
Indexer Celia McCoy

First American Edition, 2020
Published in the United States by DK Publishing
6081 E. 82nd Street, Indianapolis, Indiana 46250

22 23 24   10 9 8 7 6 5 4
004-317430-SEP2020

ISBN: 978-1-4654-9331-6
Library of Congress Catalog Number: 2020931116

Printed and bound in China

Author photo by Laura Barr.
All other images © Dorling Kindersley Limited
For further information see: www.dkimages.com

For the curious

www.dk.com

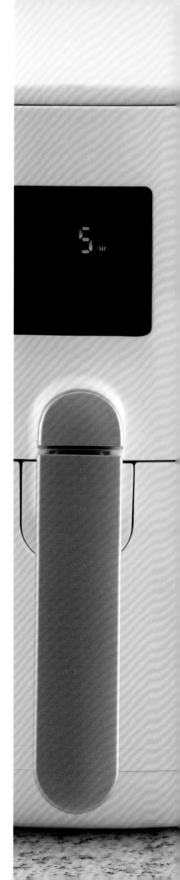

Contents

Introduction

Air frying goes vegan! I'm not an uber-experienced vegan chef, but I *am* an air fryer expert.

One of the things I've learned from years of air fryer cooking is that it's awesome for preparing vegetables and other plant-based foods. I've worked tirelessly to perfect these recipes—and truthfully surprised myself in what is possible with the air fryer when using simple, whole food ingredients. These recipes aren't designed to always be the lowest calorie options out there—I don't believe health is only about calories—but all the recipes are sensibly portioned and made with the freshest ingredients.

This collection of vegan recipes sets out to do several things: Reinvent classic recipes, create innovative new flavors, and highlight the beauty of plant-based foods. Apple Pies (pg. 150) and Banana Bread (pg. 21) demonstrate how scrumptious vegan baked goods can be. Family favorites like fried mozzarella, homemade pizza, and eggplant Parmesan have been rejuvenated with plant-based cheeses and transformed into soon-to-be new family favorites to enjoy: Faux Mozzarella Sticks (pg. 114), Personal Veggie Pizza (pg. 45), and Eggplant Casserole (pg. 42).

Some totally new creations that highlight important nutrients like omega-3 fats, tummy-pleasing fiber, and cell-protecting antioxidants include Chocolate, Orange & Chia Pudding Tarts (pg. 155), Cashew Stir-Fry (pg. 65), Yucca Fries (pg. 80), and Jackfruit Crab Cakes with Homemade Cocktail Sauce (pg. 50). And I know I'm supposed to like all of my recipe children, but Avocado Egg Rolls (pg. 101), Poppy Seed Scones with Lemon Glaze (pg. 16), Fried Green Tomato Po' Boys (pg. 47), and Kale & Veggie Sausage Wraps (pg. 24) are a few of my absolute favorites.

You don't need to follow a vegan diet to get the most out of this cookbook. Eating a plant-based diet can mean eating *more* plants, not eating *only* plants. There are no rules when it comes to plant-based eating—and there's no disputing that plants are filled with important nutrients—but let's face it: They have a reputation for being boring and they don't deserve that! I want to revamp your love for veggies and fruit as well as spark your creativity for legumes, grains, nuts, and seeds. Whether you're new to air frying or new to plant-based eating—or new to both—these recipes are for you. I can't wait for you to dive in!

Dana White

Dana Angelo White

Air Fryer Basics

Air Fryer Essentials

It can't do everything in your kitchen,
but it certainly can do some things better.

Better-for-You Cooking

There's no huge mystery to air fryers. They're
basically mini convection ovens. A powerful
fan blasts hot air around food, helping make it
extra crispy. This method is much faster than
a conventional oven and allows for food to cook
quickly and evenly. Air fryers have become
famous for finger-licking french fries (vegan)
and greaseless chicken wings (not vegan), but
they're truly ideal for all kinds of plant-based
foods—from Lentil Empanadas (pg. 66) to
Chocolate & Zucchini Muffins (pg. 29).

If you're a fan of fried foods and you're trying to cut
back on calories and fat, the air fryer can help,
allowing you to make healthier versions of potato
skins, arepas, and even donuts. This book also
features exciting salads! Yup, the air fryer helps
make the best croutons, spiced nuts, roasted
veggies, and other fun salad adornments. The
Kale Salad with Spicy Miso Dressing (pg. 130),
featuring raw and air-fried kale, is a must-try.

Tips for Success

Temperature
All air fryers are different, so don't panic if your machine shows variable settings for time and temperature. Often, the temperature adjustments are in 5-degree or 10-degree increments. If there's a temperature discrepancy with these recipes and your machine, use the lower-temp option and turn up the temp during cooking if needed. However, if you want to make one of these recipes in a conventional oven, increase the oven temp by 5 or 10 degrees Fahrenheit.

Basket Size
Air fryer basket sizes also vary significantly. For this reason, you might have to make your recipes in several batches or one large batch depending on the capacity of your machine. Just be sure not to overcrowd the basket because this will interrupt the air flow and have a negative impact on the quality of the finished dish.

Cleaning
Plant-based foods are often less greasy—no meat drippings to worry about—so that alone helps keep the machine clean and working well. Always wipe crumbs and other food particles from the machine after each use to prevent buildup, which can burn and make the machine produce smoke at high cooking temperatures.

NOTE | The recipes in this book were developed using the Bella 5.3 QT air fryer— a midrange-priced model with a spacious inner basket.

Benefits of Eating a Plant-Based Diet

Vegan diets are a hot trend, but what makes them different from other fads is that there's science to back them up.

Plant-based foods—including fruits, vegetables, legumes, nuts, seeds, oils, and grains—all play an important role in our health. Vegetarian-style diets have been linked to reduced risks of chronic illnesses, including coronary heart disease, diabetes, and certain types of cancer. These benefits are reliant on a few things—most importantly that you need to eat plant-based foods regularly. Eating only french fries or a small portion of beans once a month in your vegan diet won't expose you to the nutrients that have been found to help promote health. Eating a wide variety of plant-based foods is often the key to success.

Some of the Most Impressive Healthy Attributes of Plant-Based Foods

- Plants offer fiber, which helps promote healthy digestion and keeps you feeling fuller longer.

- Oils, nuts, and seeds are full of healthy fats that actually contribute to lower cholesterol and better heart health.

- Plant foods contain no cholesterol, but some still contain unhealthy saturated fats, which negatively impact heart health, so watch for these.

- Plant-based proteins like soy, quinoa, hemp, and chia seeds contain a full panel of amino acids— protein building blocks—the same as meat and other animal-based foods.

Vegan Swaps

Craving the texture of meat, the binding properties of eggs, or that one-of-a-kind cheesy flavor? Try these tried-and-true vegan alternatives.

Food Item	Swap
Eggs for baking	Ground flaxseed and water
Eggs for sandwiches; scrambled eggs	Crumbled tofu or liquid egg substitute, like JUST Egg
Ground meat for tacos	Chopped mushrooms or walnuts
Ground meat for burgers and sandwiches	Tempeh
Mayo/cream sauce	Soaked cashews
Parmesan cheese	Nutritional yeast or miso paste

Vegan Boosts

Looking to add nutrients to your vegan recipes? Try these.

Nutrient	Boost
Protein	Soy milk/yogurt, beans, lentils
Calcium	Leafy green veggies, tofu, fortified milks (almond, soy, etc.)
Iron	Spinach, beans, lentils, seeds, fortified cereals
Omega-3 fats	Chia seeds, walnuts, flaxseed
Zinc	Nuts, chia seeds, pumpkin seeds, beans, tofu
B-12	Nutritional yeast, tempeh, fortified dairy-free milk, fortified cereals

Breakfast

Poppy Seed Scones
with Lemon Glaze

High heat from the air fryer ensures the most delightful scones. Although they're traditionally made with butter, these scones feature coconut oil.

MAKES **4** • SERVING SIZE **1**

237 CALORIES
PER SERVING

FRYER TEMP **320°F**

PREP TIME **10 mins**

COOK TIME **12 mins**

1 cup all-purpose flour

2 tbsp granulated sugar

1½ tsp baking powder

⅛ tsp kosher salt

2 tbsp coconut oil

¼ cup unsweetened soy milk

2 tsp poppy seeds

zest of 1 lemon

FOR THE GLAZE

1½ tsp freshly squeezed lemon juice

3 tbsp powdered sugar

1. Set the air fryer temp to 320°F.

2. In a large bowl, whisk together the flour, granulated sugar, baking powder, and salt.

3. Use a pastry cutter to work the coconut oil into the flour, evenly distributing the oil throughout the dry ingredients and forming the flour into the size of small peas.

4. Add the soy milk, poppy seeds, and lemon zest. Mix gently with clean hands, being careful not to overmix. Gently press the dough into a baking dish.

5. Place the dish in the fryer basket and bake until the edges are golden, about 12 minutes.

6. Remove the dish from the basket. Allow the scones to cool for 10 minutes. Slice into triangles and transfer to a wire rack.

7. In a small bowl, make the glaze by whisking together the lemon juice and powdered sugar until thick.

8. Drizzle the glaze over the scones. Allow to set for 15 minutes before serving.

TIP | Look for butter-flavored coconut oil, such as Keto Coconut Infusions from Ellyndale Organics.

NUTRITION PER 1 SCONE:

TOTAL FAT **8g** • SATURATED FAT **6g** • CHOLESTEROL **0mg** • SODIUM **84mg** • CARBS **38g** DIETARY FIBERS **1g** • SUGARS **13g** • PROTEIN **4g**

Apricot & Oatmeal Bars

Sweetened with maple syrup and dried fruit, these granola bars can help you start your day with wholesome, simple ingredients.

250 CALORIES PER SERVING

FRYER TEMP **350°F**

PREP TIME **10 mins**

COOK TIME **10 mins**

MAKES **10** • SERVING SIZE **1**

1 cup rolled oats

½ cup crunchy almond butter

½ cup whole raw almonds

½ cup dried apricots

½ cup unsweetened dried coconut flakes

4 tbsp maple syrup

½ tsp sea salt

1. Set the air fryer temp to 350°F.

2. Place the ingredients in a food processor and pulse until well combined. Firmly and evenly press the mixture into a 7-inch (17.5cm) springform pan.

3. Place the pan in the fryer basket and bake until the edges begin to brown, about 10 minutes.

4. Remove the pan from the fryer basket and allow the granola to cool completely in the pan.

5. Remove the granola from the pan and cut it into 10 bars.

TIP | Use certified gluten-free oats to make this recipe gluten-free.

TIP | You can also cut the granola in the pan while it's still hot, then allow to cool and harden completely before removing.

NUTRITION PER 1 BAR:

TOTAL FAT **17g** • SATURATED FAT **5g** • CHOLESTEROL **0mg** • SODIUM **192mg** • CARBS **21g** DIETARY FIBERS **4g** • SUGARS **8g** • PROTEIN **6g**

Peanut Butter & Chia Breakfast Squares

202 CALORIES PER SERVING

FRYER TEMP **350°F**

PREP TIME **10 mins**

COOK TIME **10 mins**

Peanut butter for breakfast! These squares are sweet, savory, chewy, and crunchy—all the textures to satisfy your morning cravings.

MAKES **10** • SERVING SIZE **1**

1 tbsp chia seeds

2 tbsp water

1 cup rolled oats

½ cup crunchy peanut butter

½ cup unsalted pistachios

½ cup raisins

½ cup unsweetened dried coconut flakes

4 tbsp maple syrup

½ tsp sea salt

1. Set the air fryer temp to 350°F.

2. In a small bowl, combine the chia seeds and water. Set aside.

3. Place the remaining ingredients in a food processor and pulse until well combined. Add the chia seeds and pulse two or three more times until mixed in. Firmly and evenly press the mixture into a 7-inch (17.5cm) springform pan.

4. Place the pan in the fryer basket and cook until the edges begin to brown, about 10 minutes.

5. Remove the pan from the fryer basket and allow the granola to cool completely in the pan.

6. Remove the granola from the pan and cut it into 10 squares.

TIP | If you use sweetened peanut butter, use 2 tablespoons of maple syrup.

NUTRITION PER 1 SQUARE:

TOTAL FAT **12g** · SATURATED FAT **5g** · CHOLESTEROL **0mg** · SODIUM **157mg** · CARBS **22g** DIETARY FIBERS **4g** · SUGARS **11g** · PROTEIN **6g**

Banana Bread

This is the absolutely best thing to do with overripe bananas. Flaxseed and the fruit take the place of eggs in this delightful vegan sweet treat.

MAKES **8 slices** • SERVING SIZE **1 slice**

176 CALORIES PER SERVING

FRYER TEMP **310°F**

PREP TIME **10 mins**

COOK TIME **25 mins**

1 tbsp ground flaxseed

3 tbsp water

½ cup all-purpose flour

¼ cup almond flour

½ tsp ground cinnamon

½ tsp baking powder

⅛ tsp kosher salt

½ cup granulated sugar

¼ cup unsweetened almond milk

½ tsp pure vanilla extract

¼ cup canola oil

2 medium ripe bananas, mashed

½ medium ripe banana, sliced lengthwise

1. Set the air fryer temp to 310°F. Spray 2 mini loaf pans with nonstick cooking spray. Set aside.

2. In a small bowl, combine the flaxseed and water. Set aside.

3. In a large bowl, whisk together the all-purpose flour, almond flour, cinnamon, baking powder, and salt.

4. In a separate large bowl, combine the sugar, almond milk, vanilla extract, canola oil, mashed bananas, and flaxseed mixture.

5. Gently fold the wet ingredients into the dry ingredients until completely combined.

6. Place half the batter in a pan and top with a sliced banana. Repeat this step with the remaining batter and sliced banana.

7. Place the pans in the fryer basket and bake until a toothpick comes out clean from the center, about 22 to 25 minutes.

8. Remove the pans from the fryer basket. Allow the bread to cool for at least 10 minutes. Remove the bread from the pans before serving.

NUTRITION PER 1 SLICE:

TOTAL FAT **8g** • SATURATED FAT **1g** • CHOLESTEROL **0mg** • SODIUM **42mg** • CARBS **26g** DIETARY FIBERS **2g** • SUGARS **16g** • PROTEIN **2g**

Cinnamon Donut Bites

Dazzle guests (and your family) with these sweet and flaky donut bites. Make the dough the night before and pop it in the air fryer just before breakfast.

219 CALORIES PER SERVING

FRYER TEMP **370°F**

PREP TIME **10 mins**

COOK TIME **6 mins**

MAKES **12** • SERVING SIZE **3**

2 tbsp ground flaxseed

6 tbsp water

1 cup plus 2 tbsp all-purpose flour

½ tsp kosher salt

2 tsp ground cinnamon, divided

1 tsp baking powder

¼ cup light brown sugar

¼ cup unsweetened soy milk

1 tbsp melted coconut oil

¼ cup granulated sugar

1. In a small bowl, combine the flaxseed and water. Mix well.

2. In a large bowl, whisk together the flour, salt, ½ teaspoon of cinnamon, and baking powder. Add the brown sugar, soy milk, coconut oil, and flaxseed mixture. Mix until a sticky dough forms. Refrigerate the dough for at least 1 hour.

3. Set the air fryer temp to 370°F. Spray the fryer basket with nonstick cooking spray.

4. In a small bowl, combine the sugar and the remaining 1½ teaspoons of cinnamon.

5. Use a small cookie scoop to make 12 tablespoons of dough. Roll the dough into balls and then roll the dough in the cinnamon and sugar mixture.

6. Place the balls in the fryer basket and cook until puffed and golden brown, about 6 minutes.

7. Transfer the donut bites to a platter and serve immediately.

NUTRITION PER 3 BITES:

TOTAL FAT **5g** • SATURATED FAT **3g** • CHOLESTEROL **0mg** • SODIUM **304mg** • CARBS **36g** DIETARY FIBERS **2g** • SUGARS **12g** • PROTEIN **4g**

Toasted Coconut Energy Bites

These make an awesome light breakfast. Muesli is a delightful combination of grains, nuts, dried fruit, and seeds, but you can use plain rolled oats instead.

MAKES **24** • SERVING SIZE **3**

242 CALORIES
PER SERVING

FRYER TEMP **370°F**

PREP TIME **20 mins**

COOK TIME **3 mins**

1 cup unsweetened dried coconut flakes

1 cup muesli

½ cup ground flaxseed

1 tbsp chia seeds

⅓ cup vegan chocolate chips

½ tsp kosher salt

½ cup nut butter

¼ cup agave nectar

1. Set the air fryer temp to 370°F.

2. Place the coconut in a baking dish. Place the dish in the fryer basket and cook until golden around the edges, about 2 to 3 minutes.

3. Remove the dish from the fryer basket and pour the coconut onto parchment paper to cool completely.

4. In a large bowl, combine the coconut flakes, muesli, flaxseed, chia seeds, chocolate chips, and salt. Mix well. Add the nut butter and agave. Mix again. (If the mixture appears too dry, add a few more drops of agave.)

5. Use clean hands to roll the mixture into 24 balls. Place the balls in an airtight container and refrigerate for at least 30 minutes before serving. Store in the fridge or freezer for up to 1 week.

TIP Be sure to use unsweetened coconut flakes for this recipe. Sweetened varieties will burn quickly.

NUTRITION PER 3 BITES:

TOTAL FAT **15g** • SATURATED FAT **10g** • CHOLESTEROL **0mg** • SODIUM **172mg** • CARBS **26g**
DIETARY FIBERS **6g** • SUGARS **10g** • PROTEIN **4g**

Kale & Veggie "Sausage" Wraps

This delicious plant-based breakfast of champions is chock-full of fiber and protein to keep you going strong all morning long.

MAKES **2** • SERVING SIZE **1**

330 CALORIES PER SERVING

FRYER TEMP **350°F**

PREP TIME **10 mins**

COOK TIME **15 mins**

2 vegan sausage patties (MorningStar Farms recommended)

½ cup liquid egg substitute (JUST Egg recommended)

1 cup chopped kale

2 large whole wheat flour tortillas

hot sauce (Frank's RedHot recommended) (optional)

1. Set the air fryer temp to 350°F.

2. Place the sausage in a baking dish. Place the dish in the fryer basket and cook for 5 minutes.

3. Remove the dish from the basket. Dice the sausage and add the egg and kale to the dish.

4. Return the dish to the fryer basket and cook the mixture until firm, about 10 minutes more.

5. Remove the dish from the fryer basket. Slice the mixture into 8 equally sized portions. Place 4 pieces on each tortilla. Serve with the hot sauce (if using).

NUTRITION PER 1 WRAP:

TOTAL FAT **13g** • SATURATED FAT **0g** • CHOLESTEROL **0mg** • SODIUM **440mg** • CARBS **23g** DIETARY FIBERS **9g** • SUGARS **1g** • PROTEIN **20g**

Kale Frittata

Make this protein-packed meal ahead of time and then reheat. I love the way kale gets crispy in the air fryer, but you can use any veggies you have on hand.

263 CALORIES PER SERVING

FRYER TEMP **350°F**

PREP TIME **5 mins**

COOK TIME **18 mins**

MAKES **2 servings** • SERVING SIZE **1 serving**

1½ cups chopped kale

¼ cup thinly sliced red onion

1 cup liquid egg substitute (JUST Egg recommended)

½ tsp kosher salt

¼ tsp freshly ground black pepper

1. Set the air fryer temp to 350°F. Spray a baking pan with nonstick cooking spray.

2. Place the kale and onion in the pan. Place the pan in the fryer basket and cook for 3 minutes.

3. Remove the pan from the fryer basket. Add the egg, salt, and pepper. Stir gently.

4. Return the pan to the fryer basket and cook until the frittata has become firm, about 15 minutes more.

5. Transfer the frittata to a platter. Cut the frittata into 2 equally sized portions before serving.

TIP | Fancy this up for brunch guests by adding a sprinkle of shredded vegan Cheddar-style cheese for the last 2 minutes of cooking and then garnish with fresh chives.

NUTRITION PER ½ FRITTATA:

TOTAL FAT **18g** • SATURATED FAT **1g** • CHOLESTEROL **0mg** • SODIUM **501mg** • CARBS **10g**
DIETARY FIBERS **1g** • SUGARS **1g** • PROTEIN **15g**

Tofu Rancheros

These fully loaded corn tortillas have all the fixings—high-protein tofu scramble perched on a warm tortilla with piles of fresh herbs and veggies.

331 CALORIES PER SERVING

FRYER TEMP **400°F**

PREP TIME **10 mins**

COOK TIME **5 mins**

MAKES **4 tortillas** • SERVING SIZE **1 tortilla**

2 cups crumbled firm tofu

2 tsp Dijon mustard

1 tsp nutritional yeast

½ tsp ground turmeric

½ tsp kosher salt

FOR SERVING

1 cup black beans

½ cup thinly sliced radishes

1 avocado, sliced

chopped fresh cilantro

4 medium corn tortillas, warmed

hot sauce (Frank's RedHot recommended) (optional)

1. Set the air fryer temp to 400°F.

2. In a baking dish, combine the tofu, mustard, nutritional yeast, turmeric, and salt. Mix well.

3. Place the dish in the fryer basket and cook until warmed, about 5 minutes.

4. Remove the dish from the fryer basket and stir the ingredients. Place the tofu mixture, black beans, radishes, avocado, cilantro, and hot sauce (if using) on the tortillas. Serve immediately.

TIP | For crispier tortillas, cook them in the air fryer for a few minutes before filling and serving them.

NUTRITION PER 1 TORTILLA:

TOTAL FAT **17g** • SATURATED FAT **3g** • CHOLESTEROL **0mg** • SODIUM **368mg** • CARBS **34g**
DIETARY FIBERS **10g** • SUGARS **2g** • PROTEIN **16g**

Chocolate & Zucchini Muffins

These veggie muffins have become a household staple! Cocoa powder adds antioxidants—and no one will mind a few chocolate chips in their muffins.

MAKES **12** • SERVING SIZE **1**

154 CALORIES PER SERVING

FRYER TEMP **270°F**

PREP TIME **10 mins**

COOK TIME **36 mins**

1 tbsp ground flaxseed

3 tbsp water

½ cup all-purpose flour

¼ cup whole wheat pastry flour

¼ cup unsweetened cocoa powder

¼ tsp baking soda

¼ tsp kosher salt

¼ tsp ground cinnamon

½ cup granulated sugar

¼ cup canola oil

½ tsp pure vanilla extract

½ tsp freshly squeezed lemon juice

¾ cup grated zucchini

½ cup vegan chocolate chips

1. Set the air fryer temp to 270°F. Spray 12 silicone muffin cups with nonstick cooking spray. Set aside.

2. In a small bowl, combine the flaxseed and water.

3. In a large bowl, whisk together the all-purpose flour, whole wheat pastry flour, cocoa powder, baking soda, salt, and cinnamon. Add the sugar, canola oil, vanilla extract, lemon juice, and flaxseed mixture. Mix well. Fold in the zucchini and chocolate chips. Place the batter into the muffin cups.

4. Working in batches, place 6 muffin cups in the fryer basket and bake until a toothpick comes out clean from the center of a muffin, about 15 to 18 minutes.

5. Remove the cups from the fryer basket and allow the muffins to cool for 10 minutes before serving.

NUTRITION PER 1 MUFFIN:

TOTAL FAT **8g** • SATURATED FAT **1g** • CHOLESTEROL **0mg** • SODIUM **29mg** • CARBS **22g**
DIETARY FIBERS **2g** • SUGARS **8g** • PROTEIN **2g**

Black Bean Burger Burritos

In just a few minutes, you can prepare the filling for and wrap and toast these burritos. This dish features plenty of protein and fiber to keep you feeling full.

357 CALORIES PER SERVING

FRYER TEMP **380°F**

PREP TIME **10 mins**

COOK TIME **10 mins**

MAKES **4** • SERVING SIZE **1**

4 black bean burgers

sriracha chili sauce

4 large flour tortillas

baby spinach

1 avocado, diced

1. Set the air fryer temp to 380°F.

2. Place the black bean burgers in the fryer basket and cook for 4 minutes per side.

3. Remove the burgers from the fryer basket and roughly chop. Spread the chili sauce on the tortillas and top with equal amounts of spinach, avocado, and burger. Wrap the tortillas around the filling.

4. Place the burritos in the fryer basket and cook until the tortillas are toasted, about 2 minutes.

5. Remove the burritos from the fryer basket and cut in half. Serve immediately or wrap them in aluminum foil for an on-the-go meal.

NUTRITION PER 1 BURRITO:

TOTAL FAT **16g** • SATURATED FAT **3g** • CHOLESTEROL **0mg** • SODIUM **770mg** • CARBS **42g** DIETARY FIBERS **8g** • SUGARS **2g** • PROTEIN **16g**

Breakfast Sandwiches

This eggless sandwich—piled high with veggie sausage, soy cheese, and avocado tucked into mini bagels—will give your morning a quick boost.

MAKES **4** • SERVING SIZE **1**

352 CALORIES
PER SERVING

FRYER TEMP **400°F**

PREP TIME **5 mins**

COOK TIME **8 mins**

4 mini bagels, sliced

4 veggie sausage patties

4 slices soy cheese

1 avocado, sliced

1. Set the air fryer temp to 400°F.

2. Place the bagels cut side up and the sausage patties in the fryer basket. Cook until the bagels are toasted, about 4 minutes.

3. Pause the machine and remove the bagels. Set aside.

4. Top each patty with 1 slice of cheese. Restart the machine and cook for 4 minutes more.

5. Transfer each patty to between 2 bagel halves. Top each patty with avocado slices and serve immediately.

NUTRITION PER 1 SANDWICH:

TOTAL FAT **16g** • SATURATED FAT **4g** • CHOLESTEROL **0mg** • SODIUM **633mg** • CARBS **29g** DIETARY FIBERS **8g** • SUGARS **3g** • PROTEIN **17g**

3-Ingredient Everything Bagels

156 CALORIES PER SERVING

FRYER TEMP **320°F**

PREP TIME **10 mins**

COOK TIME **12 mins**

After 3-ingredient bagels (made with yogurt) broke the Internet, I wanted to make a plant-based version. These are flakier—and divine with sliced avocado.

MAKES **4** • SERVING SIZE **1**

1 cup all-purpose flour, plus more

2 tsp baking powder

½ tsp kosher salt

5oz (150g) unsweetened dairy-free yogurt (soy recommended)

everything bagel seasoning

1. Set the air fryer temp to 320°F.

2. In a large bowl, whisk together the flour, baking powder, and salt. Add the yogurt and stir with a spatula until a loose dough forms.

3. Turn the dough out onto a lightly floured surface. Gently knead the dough until it comes together.

4. Divide the dough in half and then into 4 equally sized pieces. Roll each piece of dough into a ball and gently press to flatten.

5. Cut a hole in the center using a small ring mold or a butter knife. Spray the top of the dough with nonstick cooking spray. Sprinkle 1 to 2 teaspoons of seasoning over the top of each disc.

6. Place the dough in the fryer basket and bake until puffed and golden brown, about 12 minutes.

7. Transfer the bagels to a wire rack to cool slightly before serving. Slice, toast, and top as desired.

TIP | For a slightly sweeter flavor, use vanilla yogurt.

NUTRITION PER 1 BAGEL:

TOTAL FAT **4g** • SATURATED FAT **1g** • CHOLESTEROL **0mg** • SODIUM **294mg** • CARBS **25g** DIETARY FIBERS **1g** • SUGARS **0g** • PROTEIN **5g**

Blueberry & Orange French Toast Casserole

This is the ultimate comfort breakfast—made even better with blueberries and faster with the air fryer. This lighter version is a great low-calorie breakfast.

300 CALORIES PER SERVING

FRYER TEMP **350°F**

PREP TIME **10 mins**

COOK TIME **15 mins**

MAKES **2 servings** • SERVING SIZE **1 serving**

4 slices vegan bread (whole grain recommended), cubed

1 cup blueberries

1 tbsp ground flaxseed

3 tbsp water

1 cup unsweetened vanilla almond milk

1 tsp pure vanilla extract

2 tbsp maple syrup, plus more

1 tbsp orange zest

1. Set the air fryer temp to 350°F. Spray a baking dish with nonstick cooking spray.

2. Place the bread and blueberries in the dish. Set aside.

3. In a small bowl, combine the flaxseed and water. Mix well.

4. In a medium bowl, whisk together the almond milk, vanilla extract, maple syrup, orange zest, and flaxseed mixture. Pour the liquid mixture over the bread and blueberries. Gently press down on the bread to submerge.

5. Place the dish in the fryer basket and bake until the edges are golden brown and the center is firm, about 15 minutes.

6. Remove the dish from the fryer basket and allow the casserole to cool for 10 minutes. Spoon out 2 equally sized portions and drizzle more maple syrup over the top before serving.

TIP | Don't have blueberries? Use any type of seasonal berry or diced plums or peaches.

NUTRITION PER 1 SERVING:

TOTAL FAT **5g** • SATURATED FAT **0g** • CHOLESTEROL **0mg** • SODIUM **375mg** • CARBS **65g**
DIETARY FIBERS **13g** • SUGARS **21g** • PROTEIN **12g**

Breakfast Arepas

These stuffed corn cakes are inspired by my favorite Venezuelan restaurant. This is a veggie and bean version, but you can also fill it with scrambled tofu.

MAKES **4** • SERVING SIZE **1**

264 CALORIES
PER SERVING

FRYER TEMP **380°F**

PREP TIME **10 mins**

COOK TIME **15 mins**

2 tsp plus 1 tbsp olive oil

¼ cup diced red onion

¼ cup diced bell pepper (any color)

½ tsp ground cumin

1½ tsp kosher salt, divided

¼ cup canned black beans, rinsed and drained

1 cup masarepa cornmeal

1 cup water

1. Set the air fryer temp to 380°F.

2. In a small skillet on the stovetop over medium heat, warm 2 teaspoons of olive oil. Add the onion and pepper. Sauté until slightly tender, about 5 minutes.

3. Stir in the cumin, ½ teaspoon of salt, and beans. Remove the skillet from the heat and set aside to cool slightly.

4. In a medium bowl, combine the cornmeal, water, and the remaining 1 teaspoon of salt. Mix until a soft dough forms.

5. Form the dough into a ball and divide into 4 equally sized pieces. Divide each piece in half and form each half into a small disc. Place 2 tablespoons of filling in the center of each disc. Place the remaining discs on top and gently press the edges closed. Brush the discs on both sides with the remaining 1 tablespoon of olive oil.

6. Place the discs in the fryer basket and cook until crispy, about 15 minutes.

7. Transfer the arepas to a platter and allow to cool slightly before serving.

TIP | You can cook the red onion and bell pepper in the air fryer instead. In a baking dish, combine the onion, pepper, and 2 teaspoons of olive oil. Place the dish in the fryer basket and cook for 2 to 3 minutes. Remove the dish from the fryer basket and set aside to cool.

TIP | Serve these along with a fruit smoothie for a more complete meal.

NUTRITION PER 1 AREPA:
TOTAL FAT **6g** • SATURATED FAT **0g** • CHOLESTEROL **0mg** • SODIUM **647mg** • CARBS **52g**
DIETARY FIBERS **2g** • SUGARS **1g** • PROTEIN **7g**

Mango & Yogurt Parfaits
with Toasted Walnuts

Add a healthy dose of crunch and omega-3s to your breakfast with toasty walnuts layered with tangy mango and coconut milk yogurt.

MAKES **4** • SERVING SIZE **1**

413 CALORIES PER SERVING

FRYER TEMP **320°F**

PREP TIME **5 mins**

COOK TIME **10 mins**

⅔ cup walnuts

pinch of kosher salt

¼ tsp ground cinnamon

1 tbsp maple syrup

4 cups coconut milk yogurt

2 large mangoes, peeled and diced

1. Set the air fryer temp to 320°F.

2. In a small bowl, combine the walnuts, salt, cinnamon, and maple syrup. Toss well to coat.Place the walnut mixture in a baking dish.

3. Place the dish in the fryer basket and toast for 10 minutes, tossing once halfway through.

4. Remove the dish from the fryer basket and pour the nuts onto a piece of parchment paper. Allow them to cool completely.

5. In 4 parfait glasses, alternate layers of yogurt, mango, and nuts. Refrigerate for 5 minutes before serving.

TIP | Use any dairy-free yogurt you prefer: Soy is highest in protein, almond milk is a little lighter, and coconut is rich and creamy.

TIP | You can make the nuts up to 5 days in advance and store them in an airtight container.

NUTRITION PER 1 PARFAIT:

TOTAL FAT **20g** • SATURATED FAT **2g** • CHOLESTEROL **0mg** • SODIUM **51mg** • CARBS **23g** DIETARY FIBERS **5g** • SUGARS **13g** • PROTEIN **9g**

Agave & Pistachio Granola

162 CALORIES PER SERVING

FRYER TEMP **320°F**

PREP TIME **10 mins**

COOK TIME **10 mins**

Just a little of this granola goes a long way. Adding a few spoonfuls to everything from oatmeal to salads can add the right amount of crunchy sweetness.

MAKES **2 cups** • SERVING SIZE **¼ cup**

1 cup rolled oats

½ cup shelled pistachios

¼ cup pumpkin seeds

¼ cup unsweetened dried coconut chips

2 tbsp agave nectar

2 tbsp canola or grapeseed oil

½ tsp kosher salt

½ tsp ground cinnamon

1. Set the air fryer temp to 320°F.

2. In a food processor, combine the ingredients. Pulse until small clusters have formed. Transfer the mixture to a baking dish.

3. Place the dish in the fryer basket and cook until toasted and slightly golden brown, about 10 minutes. Pause the machine every 2 to 3 minutes to stir the mixture.

4. Transfer the granola to a sheet pan lined with parchment paper to cool completely before serving.

TIP | Store the granola in an airtight container for up to 5 days.

TIP | Make this recipe gluten-free by using certified gluten-free oats.

NUTRITION PER ¼ CUP:

TOTAL FAT **10g** • SATURATED FAT **3g** • CHOLESTEROL **0mg** • SODIUM **107mg** • CARBS **15g** DIETARY FIBERS **2g** • SUGARS **5g** • PROTEIN **4g**

Sweet Potato Hash

Serve this hash in a grain bowl for a complete meal. I often finish this dish with a squeeze of fresh lime or a few dashes of hot sauce.

150 CALORIES PER SERVING

FRYER TEMP **360°F**

PREP TIME **10 mins**

COOK TIME **16 mins**

MAKES **4 servings** • SERVING SIZE **1 serving**

2 large sweet potatoes, unpeeled

½ small yellow onion, cut into large chunks

1 poblano pepper, cut into large chunks

1 cup sliced mushrooms

1 tsp kosher salt

1 tbsp olive oil

1. Microwave the sweet potatoes until softened but not completely cooked, about 3 to 4 minutes. Set aside to cool for 10 minutes.

2. Set the air fryer temp to 360°F.

3. Remove the skins from the sweet potatoes and cut the potatoes into large chunks.

4. In a medium bowl, combine the sweet potatoes, onion, pepper, mushrooms, salt, and olive oil. Toss gently to coat.

5. Place the vegetables in the fryer basket and cook for 8 minutes. Pause the machine, shake the basket, and cook for 8 minutes more.

6. Transfer the hash to a serving bowl and serve immediately.

TIP | Add black beans or roasted tofu for a protein boost.

TIP | You can make this ahead of time, store in the fridge, and eat all week.

NUTRITION PER 1 SERVING:

TOTAL FAT **4g** • SATURATED FAT **1g** • CHOLESTEROL **0mg** • SODIUM **353mg** • CARBS **28g**
DIETARY FIBERS **4g** • SUGARS **6g** • PROTEIN **3g**

Mains

Eggplant Casserole

This deconstructed spin on eggplant Parmesan comes from my rush to get dinner on the table, but I hope you love it as much as my family does.

496 **CALORIES** PER SERVING

FRYER TEMP **400°F**

PREP TIME **35 mins**

COOK TIME **23 mins**

MAKES **2 servings** • SERVING SIZE **1 serving**

1 large eggplant, peeled and diced

1 tbsp olive oil

½ tsp dried oregano

1 tsp kosher salt

¼ tsp freshly ground black pepper

1½ cups marinara sauce

½ cup vegan ricotta-style cheese

¾ cup shredded vegan mozzarella-style cheese (Daiya recommended)

3 tbsp panko breadcrumbs

1. Set the air fryer temp to 400°F. Spray a baking pan with nonstick cooking spray. Set aside.

2. In a large bowl, combine the eggplant, olive oil, oregano, salt, and pepper. Toss well to coat.

3. Place the eggplant in the fryer basket and cook until tender and starting to brown, about 10 minutes. Remove the eggplant from the fryer basket and be sure to clean out any pieces of eggplant.

4. Place half the eggplant in the pan and top with half the marinara sauce, ricotta, and mozzarella. Repeat with the remaining eggplant, sauce, and cheeses.

5. Place the pan in the fryer basket and bake for 10 minutes.

6. Remove the pan from the fryer basket and top the casserole with the breadcrumbs.

7. Return the pan to the fryer basket and cook until the breadcrumbs are golden brown, about 2 to 3 minutes more.

8. Remove the pan from the fryer basket and allow the casserole to cool for 5 to 10 minutes before serving.

TIP | To make your own vegan ricotta cheese, in a blender, combine 1 cup of soaked raw almonds, ¼ cup of firm tofu, ½ cup of water, 1 teaspoon of nutritional yeast, the juice of ½ lemon, and ¼ teaspoon of kosher salt.

NUTRITION PER 1 SERVING:

TOTAL FAT **24g** • SATURATED FAT **3g** • CHOLESTEROL **0mg** • SODIUM **717mg** • CARBS **62g**
DIETARY FIBERS **15g** • SUGARS **25g** • PROTEIN **12g**

Stuffed Spaghetti Squash

Such an easy and versatile recipe is made even easier in the air fryer. Pack this roasted winter squash with fresh veggies and other goodies.

MAKES **2 halves** • SERVING SIZE **1 half**

143 CALORIES
PER SERVING

FRYER TEMP **390°F**

PREP TIME **15 mins**

COOK TIME **40 mins**

1 small spaghetti squash, halved and seeds removed

4 tsp olive oil

1 tsp kosher salt

1 tsp freshly ground black pepper

FOR THE FILLING

baby spinach

diced tomatoes

black or Kalamata olives

sautéed mushrooms

sun-dried tomatoes

chopped pistachios

shredded vegan mozzarella-style cheese (Daiya recommended)

marinara sauce

balsamic vinaigrette

1. Set the air fryer temp to 390°F.

2. Drizzle each squash half with 2 teaspoons of olive oil. Sprinkle ½ teaspoon of salt and pepper on each half.

3. Working in batches, place 1 squash half cut side up in the fryer basket and cook until tender and the edges are golden brown, about 20 minutes.

4. Transfer the halves to a platter. Add the recommended fillings or fill the squash as desired. Serve immediately.

TIP | For a heartier meal, add cooked brown rice to the filling.

NUTRITION PER 1 HALF:

TOTAL FAT **9g** • SATURATED FAT **1g** • CHOLESTEROL **0mg** • SODIUM **316mg** • CARBS **14g** DIETARY FIBERS **0g** • SUGARS **0g** • PROTEIN **2g**

Personal Veggie Pizza

You don't need takeout when you have an air fryer. These homemade personal pizzas are your healthy answer for a crowd-pleasing meal.

345 CALORIES PER SERVING

FRYER TEMP **380°F**

PREP TIME **5 mins**

COOK TIME **48 mins**

MAKES **4** • SERVING SIZE **1**

8oz (225g) prepared pizza dough

½ cup marinara sauce

1 cup shredded vegan mozzarella-style cheese (Daiya recommended)

4 cups sliced veggies (peppers and onions recommended)

chopped fresh basil

1. Set the air fryer temp to 380°F.

2. Roll out the dough into 4 equally sized rounds. Working in batches, place a round in the fryer basket. Top each round with an equal amount of sauce, cheese, veggies, and basil. Bake until the crust is crispy and the edges are golden brown, about 10 to 12 minutes.

3. Transfer the pizzas to plates and serve immediately.

TIP | Make frozen pizza! Cook the crust ahead of time for 3 minutes and set aside to cool. Add the toppings and store the pizza in the freezer. Reheat in the air fryer for 12 to 15 minutes.

TIP | Give this pizza a different spin with barbecue sauce, shredded vegan Cheddar-style cheese, and sliced mushrooms.

NUTRITION PER 1 PIZZA:

TOTAL FAT **5g** • SATURATED FAT **1g** • CHOLESTEROL **0mg** • SODIUM **480mg** • CARBS **65g**
DIETARY FIBERS **6g** • SUGARS **3g** • PROTEIN **11g**

Fried Green Tomato Po' Boys

353 CALORIES PER SERVING

FRYER TEMP **400°F**

PREP TIME **15 mins**

COOK TIME **20 mins**

Fried green tomatoes are a summertime treasure, but I loathe the hot oil (and all those calories!). This eggless version crisps to golden perfection.

MAKES **4** • SERVING SIZE **1**

¼ cup vegan mayonnaise or **Lemon & Garlic Aioli** (pg. 78)

2 tbsp unsweetened soy milk

1 cup panko breadcrumbs

½ tsp smoked paprika

2 green tomatoes, thickly sliced

FOR SERVING

vegan mayonnaise or **Lemon & Garlic Aioli** (pg. 78)

4 vegan sandwich rolls

pickles

arugula

1. Set the air fryer temp to 400°F. Spray the fryer basket with nonstick cooking spray.

2. In a small bowl, whisk together the mayonnaise and soy milk.

3. In a separate small bowl, combine the breadcrumbs and paprika.

4. Pat the tomato slices dry with paper towels to remove any excess liquid. Dip the slices in the mayo mixture and flip to coat both sides. Transfer them to the breadcrumb mixture and flip to coat both sides.

5. Working in batches, place half the tomato slices in the fryer basket. Cook until the breadcrumbs are crispy and golden brown, about 8 to 10 minutes.

6. Transfer the tomato slices to a plate. Spread a thin layer of mayonnaise on the rolls and top with 2 tomato slices, pickles, and arugula. Serve immediately.

TIP | You can also make this with sliced eggplant.

NUTRITION PER 1 PO' BOY:

TOTAL FAT **14g** • SATURATED FAT **2g** • CHOLESTEROL **0mg** • SODIUM **864mg** • CARBS **50g** DIETARY FIBERS **7g** • SUGARS **10g** • PROTEIN **9g**

Tempeh Banh Mi

This recipe was inspired by a sandwich I once had that was made with pork belly. Tempeh is the perfect plant-based swap in my vegan spin on this classic.

MAKES **4 sandwiches** • SERVING SIZE **1 sandwich**

416 CALORIES PER SERVING

FRYER TEMP **400°F**

PREP TIME **30 mins**

COOK TIME **10 mins**

2 tbsp gluten-free tamari or reduced-sodium soy sauce

1 tbsp ketchup

1 tbsp rice vinegar

8oz (225g) tempeh, sliced into 12 pieces

FOR SERVING

4 vegan sandwich rolls or baguettes, toasted

vegan mayonnaise

sriracha chili sauce

baby green leaf lettuce

shredded carrots

Pickled Onions (pg. 55)

1. In a shallow dish, whisk together the tamari, ketchup, and rice vinegar. Add the tempeh and marinate for at least 30 minutes or up to overnight in the fridge. Once marinated, pat dry with paper towels.

2. Set the air fryer temp to 400°F. Spray the fryer basket with nonstick cooking spray.

3. Place the tempeh in the fryer basket and cook until the edges are crispy, about 8 to 10 minutes.

4. Transfer the tempeh to a plate. Spread the mayo on the rolls and drizzle the chili sauce over the mayo. Layer 3 pieces of tempeh on each sandwich and top with the lettuce, carrots, and Pickled Onions. Serve immediately.

TIP | Toast the bread in the air fryer at 400°F for 2 to 3 minutes.

NUTRITION PER 1 SANDWICH:

TOTAL FAT **13g** • SATURATED FAT **2g** • CHOLESTEROL **0mg** • SODIUM **634mg** • CARBS **61g**

DIETARY FIBERS **8g** • SUGARS **10g** • PROTEIN 20G

Balsamic Mushroom Burgers

These low-calorie burgers are just as juicy and scrumptious as their meaty counterparts. Hummus adds flavor and protein to this plant-based meal.

MAKES **4** • SERVING SIZE **1**

309 CALORIES PER SERVING

FRYER TEMP **400°F**

PREP TIME **25 mins**

COOK TIME **8 mins**

3 tbsp balsamic vinegar

1 tbsp reduced-sodium soy sauce

1 tsp Dijon mustard

2 garlic cloves, minced

4 portobello mushroom caps, stems removed and gills scooped out

4 vegan hamburger buns, toasted

½ cup hummus

1 red onion, sliced

1 avocado, sliced

butter or green leaf lettuce

1. In a large bowl, whisk together the balsamic vinegar, soy sauce, mustard, and garlic. Brush the mushrooms with the sauce and allow to marinate for 10 minutes.

2. Set the air fryer temp to 400°F.

3. Place the mushrooms in the fryer basket and cook until hot and slighly charred at the edges, about 8 minutes, turning once halfway through. Allow to cool in the fryer basket for 2 to 3 minutes.

4. Slather the buns with the hummus and fill with an equal amount of the mushrooms, onion, avocado, and lettuce. Serve immediately.

NUTRITION PER 1 BURGER:

TOTAL FAT **15g** • SATURATED FAT **3g** • CHOLESTEROL **0mg** • SODIUM **479mg** • CARBS **36g**
DIETARY FIBERS **8g** • SUGARS **4g** • PROTEIN **11g**

Jackfruit "Crab" Cakes
with Homemade Cocktail Sauce

Jackfruit is a great plant-based alternative for crab: easy to work with, mildly flavored, insanely yummy— and can transform into pulled pork or these cakes.

134 CALORIES PER SERVING

FRYER TEMP **400°F**

PREP TIME **10 mins**

COOK TIME **12 mins**

MAKES **6** • SERVING SIZE **1**

20oz (560g) canned jackfruit, rinsed, drained, and patted dry

1 slice whole grain bread

3 tbsp unsweetened soy milk

2 tbsp vegan mayonnaise

3 tbsp finely chopped celery

1 tbsp Old Bay Seasoning

½ tsp garlic powder

5 tbsp panko breadcrumbs

lemon wedges

FOR THE SAUCE

¼ cup ketchup

2 tsp horseradish

1. Set the air fryer temp to 400°F. Spray the fryer basket with canola oil.

2. Make the cocktail sauce in a small bowl by combining the ketchup and horseradish. Set aside.

3. Roughly chop the jackfruit and discard any hard pieces. Place the jackfruit in a medium bowl. Set aside.

4. In a separate medium bowl, place the bread and soy milk. Allow the bread to soak up the milk.

5. Add the bread, milk, mayonnaise, celery, Old Bay Seasoning, garlic powder, and breadcrumbs to the jackfruit. Mix well. With clean hands, form the mixture into 6 equally sized cakes.

6. Place the cakes in the fryer basket and cook until golden brown, about 12 minutes.

7. Transfer the cakes to a serving platter. Serve immediately with the cocktail sauce and lemon wedges.

TIP | You can find jackfruit canned in a brine at Trader Joe's.

NUTRITION PER 1 CRAB CAKE:

TOTAL FAT **5g** • SATURATED FAT **1g** • CHOLESTEROL **0mg** • SODIUM **298mg** • CARBS **22g**
DIETARY FIBERS **2g** • SUGARS **14g** • PROTEIN **3g**

Tater Tot Casserole

Topping a casserole with tater tots is a brilliant hack dating back decades. This healthier veggie-based version lets you love this recipe again.

265 CALORIES PER SERVING

FRYER TEMP **400°F**

PREP TIME **15 mins**

COOK TIME **15 mins**

MAKES **4 servings** • SERVING SIZE **1 serving**

10oz (285g) vegan frozen tater tots

1 tbsp vegan butter (Earth Balance recommended)

1 tbsp all-purpose flour

½ cup unsweetened soy milk

¾ tsp kosher salt

2 cups mixed vegetables (fresh or frozen and thawed)

½ cup shredded vegan Cheddar-style cheese

1. Set the air fryer temp to 400°F. Spray a baking dish with nonstick cooking spray. Set aside.

2. Place the tater tots in the fryer basket and cook for 5 minutes. Transfer the tater tots to a bowl and set aside. Clean out any crumbs from the fryer basket.

3. In a small saucepan on the stovetop over medium heat, melt the butter. Add the flour and cook for 2 to 3 minutes. Whisk in the soy milk. Add the salt and vegetables. Mix well.

4. Place the vegetable mixture in the dish and top with the partially cooked tater tots.

5. Place the dish in the fryer basket and cook for 5 minutes. Pause the machine and sprinkle the cheese over the top. Restart the machine and bake for 5 minutes more.

6. Remove the dish from the fryer basket and allow the casserole to cool for 10 minutes before serving.

TIP | For a protein boost, add edamame, chickpeas, or crumbled soy chorizo to the filling.

NUTRITION PER 1 SERVING:

TOTAL FAT **12g** • SATURATED FAT **3g** • CHOLESTEROL **0mg** • SODIUM **567mg** • CARBS **35g**
DIETARY FIBERS **7g** • SUGARS **1g** • PROTEIN **4g**

"Chorizo" & Chickpea Lettuce Cups

Lettuce cups are the pinnacle of healthy handheld meals. These are piled high with spicy soy chorizo and topped with fresh veggies.

275 CALORIES
PER SERVING

FRYER TEMP **380°F**

PREP TIME **10 mins**

COOK TIME **14 mins**

MAKES **12** • SERVING SIZE **3**

12oz (340g) soy chorizo, casing removed (Trader Joe's recommended)

15oz (420g) canned chickpeas, rinsed and drained

½ tsp ground cumin

12 lettuce leaves (chopped iceberg lettuce or Bibb lettuce recommended)

chopped fresh cilantro

1 cup grated carrots

pickled jalapeños or **Pickled Onions** (optional) (pg. 55)

THE Green Sauce (pg. 66) (optional)

1. Set the air fryer temp to 380°F.

2. Combine the chorizo, chickpeas, and cumin in a baking dish. Place the dish in the fryer basket and cook until hot and the chorizo is slightly crispy, about 12 to 14 minutes. Pause the machine once or twice to stir the mixture.

3. Remove the dish from the fryer basket. Spoon the filling into the lettuce leaves and top with cilantro, carrots, and jalapeños (if using). Serve immediately with THE Green Sauce (if using).

TIP | Set up a lettuce cup bar with all kinds of toppings for your friends and family to DIY.

NUTRITION PER 3 LETTUCE CUPS:

TOTAL FAT **12g** • SATURATED FAT **2g** • CHOLESTEROL **0mg** • SODIUM **634mg** • CARBS **32g**
DIETARY FIBERS **10g** • SUGARS **8g** • PROTEIN **15g**

Chickpea Burgers
with Pickled Onions

Sink your teeth into this legume-loving burger, which features plenty of hunger-fighting protein and fiber, plus 25% of your daily iron needs.

MAKES **4** • SERVING SIZE **1**

340 CALORIES PER SERVING

FRYER TEMP **380°F**

PREP TIME **15 mins**

COOK TIME **15 mins**

2 tsp olive oil, plus more

½ white onion, diced

2 tsp kosher salt, divided

1 tsp freshly ground black pepper

15oz (420g) canned chickpeas, drained (not rinsed), liquid reserved

½ cup grated carrots

½ cup fresh parsley leaves, chopped

1 garlic clove, chopped

¾ tsp ground cumin

1 tsp Dijon mustard

1 tbsp tahini

¼ cup all-purpose flour, plus more

FOR THE ONIONS

¼ cup water

2 tbsp rice vinegar

1 tbsp granulated sugar

1 tsp kosher salt

½ red onion, thinly sliced

1. Set the air fryer temp to 380°F.

2. In a small saucepan on the stovetop over medium heat, make the pickled onions by combining the water, rice vinegar, sugar, and salt. Bring to a boil. Add the red onion and turn off the heat. Set aside.

3. In a medium skillet on the stovetop over medium heat, warm the olive oil. Add the white onion and season with 1 teaspoon of salt and pepper. Sauté until softened, about 2 to 3 minutes.

4. In a food processor, combine the white onion, chickpeas, carrots, parsley, garlic, cumin, mustard, tahini, flour, and the remaining 1 teaspoon of salt. Pulse until just combined. (If the mixture seems too dry, add the reserved chickpea liquid 1 tablespoon at a time.)

5. Form the mixture into 4 equally sized burgers. Transfer them to a plate that's been dusted with flour. Brush the burgers with olive oil.

6. Place the burgers in the fryer basket and cook until golden brown, about 15 minutes.

7. Remove the burgers from the fryer basket. Serve on toasted vegan whole grain buns with the pickled red onions, arugula, sliced tomatoes, **Lemon & Garlic Aioli** (pg. 78), and other desired toppings.

TIP | You can make the pickled red onions ahead of time and store them in the fridge for up to 1 week.

TIP | To make this gluten-free, swap the flour with gluten-free baking mix.

NUTRITION PER 1 BURGER:

TOTAL FAT **8g** • SATURATED FAT **1g** • CHOLESTEROL **0mg** • SODIUM **637mg** • CARBS **57g**
DIETARY FIBERS **7g** • SUGARS **5g** • PROTEIN **13g**

Tofu Kebabs
with Peanut Sauce

With high-protein tofu, tender veggies, and a creamy peanut sauce, these kebabs are intensely satisfying but won't weigh you down.

MAKES **6** • SERVING SIZE **1**

150 CALORIES PER SERVING

FRYER TEMP **400°F**

PREP TIME **10 mins**

COOK TIME **10 mins**

16oz (450g) extra-firm tofu, drained

2 red bell peppers, cut into 1½-inch (3.75cm) pieces

1 red onion, cut into 1½-inch (3.75cm) pieces

2 tbsp reduced-sodium soy sauce

FOR THE SAUCE

3 tbsp creamy peanut butter

2 tbsp reduced-sodium soy sauce

2 tbsp water

1 tbsp rice vinegar

1 tsp agave nectar

1 tsp crushed garlic

1. Slice the tofu into 4 large, flat pieces. Wrap the tofu in a towel and place a large pot on top of the towel for 15 minutes to help remove any excess water. Cut the tofu into 1½-inch (3.75cm) pieces.

2. Set the air fryer temp to 400°F.

3. In a large bowl, combine the tofu, peppers, onion, and soy sauce. Toss well to coat. Thread the tofu, pepper, and onion pieces onto bamboo skewers in alternating order.

4. Place the skewers in the fryer basket and cook until the vegetables are tender and the tofu is golden brown and crispy around the edges, about 8 to 10 minutes.

5. In a medium bowl, make the peanut sauce by whisking together the ingredients.

6. Transfer the kebabs to a platter and serve immediately with the peanut sauce.

TIP | Add a splash of sriracha for a fiery peanut sauce.

TIP | Use paper lollipop sticks instead of bamboo skewers. They fit perfectly in most air fryer baskets. You can find them online and at craft stores.

NUTRITION PER 1 KEBAB:

TOTAL FAT **8g** • SATURATED FAT **1g** • CHOLESTEROL **0mg** • SODIUM **464mg** • CARBS **11g**
DIETARY FIBERS **2g** • SUGARS **3g** • PROTEIN **12g**

Sweet & Sour Tofu & Pineapple

398 CALORIES PER SERVING

FRYER TEMP **400°F**

PREP TIME **15 mins**

COOK TIME **15 mins**

Crispy tofu glazed with a fiery sweet and sour sauce contains a lot less fat and sugar than restaurant versions of sweet and sour dishes.

MAKES **4 servings** • SERVING SIZE **1 serving**

2 tbsp chili paste (sambal oelek recommended)

¼ cup water

2 tbsp white vinegar

½ tsp chopped garlic

¼ cup granulated sugar

½ tsp kosher salt

14oz (400g) extra-firm tofu

1 tbsp cornstarch

1½ cups diced pineapple

4 cups cooked brown rice

1. Set the air fryer temp to 400°F. Spray the fryer basket with nonstick cooking spray.

2. In a blender, combine the chili paste, water, vinegar, garlic, sugar, and salt. Blend until the sugar is dissolved.

3. Transfer the mixture to a small saucepan on the stovetop over medium heat. Bring to a simmer and cook for 10 minutes to thicken. Set aside.

4. Dice the tofu and remove the liquid by gently pressing with paper towels or a clean dish towel.

5. In a medium bowl, combine the tofu and cornstarch. Gently toss.

6. Place the tofu in the fryer basket and cook for 10 minutes. Pause the machine and add the pineapple. Restart the machine and cook until the pineapple is warm and the tofu is golden and crispy, about 5 minutes more.

7. Transfer the mixture to a serving bowl. Add half the chili sauce and toss well to coat. Serve immediately with the brown rice and the remaining sauce.

TIP | For a recipe mashup, combine this with the **Cashew Stir-Fry** (pg. 65).

NUTRITION PER 1 SERVING + 1 CUP OF BROWN RICE:

TOTAL FAT **7g** • SATURATED FAT **1g** • CHOLESTEROL **0mg** • SODIUM **404mg** • CARBS **72g**
DIETARY FIBERS **6g** • SUGARS **21g** • PROTEIN **14g**

Olive & Refried Bean Taquitos

313 CALORIES
PER SERVING

FRYER TEMP **340°F**

PREP TIME **10 mins**

COOK TIME **10 mins**

Enjoy this spin on a fried taco by using cook-quality vegan canned refried beans. Make this recipe gluten-free by using corn tortillas.

MAKES **12** • SERVING SIZE **3**

6oz (170g) pitted black olives, sliced

juice of ½ lime

1 tsp ground cumin

15oz (420g) vegetarian refried beans (Trader Joe's recommended)

12 small flour tortillas, warmed

guacamole (optional)

1. Set the air fryer temp to 340°F.

2. In a small bowl, combine the olives, lime juice, and cumin.

3. Place 2 tablespoons of refried beans in the center of each tortilla. Sprinkle some of the olive mixture over the top. Roll up each tortilla, tucking the edges under the bottom to seal.Spray the tortillas with nonstick canola oil.

4. Working in batches, place 6 taquitos in the fryer basket and cook until golden brown, about 4 to 5 minutes.

5. Transfer the taquitos to a platter. Serve immediately with the guacamole (if using).

TIP | For a quick and easy guacamole, mash together 2 ripe avocados, the juice of 1 lime, a pinch of kosher salt, and 3 dashes of hot sauce.

TIP | To make the tortillas easy to roll, warm them ahead of time.

NUTRITION PER 3 TAQUITOS:

TOTAL FAT **8g** • SATURATED FAT **1g** • CHOLESTEROL **0mg** • SODIUM **623mg** • CARBS **50g**
DIETARY FIBERS **5g** • SUGARS **3g** • PROTEIN **8g**

Spanish Rice Taquitos

353 CALORIES PER SERVING

FRYER TEMP **340°F**

PREP TIME **15 mins**

COOK TIME **8 mins**

Flavorful whole grain rice is tucked into corn tortillas and then air fried. For an even bigger flavor boost, add some fresh cilantro or a thinly sliced red onion.

MAKES **12** • SERVING SIZE **3**

1 cup cooked brown rice, warmed

1 packet Sazón Goya seasoning

½ cup frozen green peas

12 medium corn tortillas

1 red bell pepper, sliced into 12 strips

guacamole

1. Set the air fryer temp to 340°F. Spray the fryer basket with nonstick canola oil.

2. In a small bowl, combine the brown rice, seasoning, and peas. Mix well.

3. Spread 2 tablespoons of the rice mixture in the center of each tortilla. Add a bell pepper strip to each tortilla. Roll up the tortillas, tucking the edges under to seal.

4. Working in batches, place 6 tortillas in the fryer basket and cook until golden brown, about 3 to 4 minutes.

5. Transfer the taquitos to a platter and serve immediately with the guacamole.

NUTRITION PER 3 TAQUITOS:

TOTAL FAT **4g** • SATURATED FAT **0g** • CHOLESTEROL **0mg** • SODIUM **173mg** • CARBS **72g**
DIETARY FIBERS **8g** • SUGARS **3g** • PROTEIN **9g**

Bowtie Pasta Bake

Layered with vegetables, pasta sauce, and cheese, this dish makes a light lunch or dinner. For an extra protein boost, add some cannellini beans.

293 CALORIES PER SERVING

FRYER TEMP **370°F**

PREP TIME **20 mins**

COOK TIME **8 mins**

MAKES **4 servings** • SERVING SIZE **1 serving**

8oz (225g) bowtie pasta (makes 4 cups cooked)

2 cups roasted vegetables (see tip)

1 cup marinara sauce

⅓ cup shredded vegan mozzarella-style cheese (Daiya recommended)

½ tsp dried oregano

1. Set the air fryer temp to 370°F.

2. Cook the pasta according to the package directions. Drain well.

3. In a large bowl, combine the pasta, roasted vegetables, and marinara sauce. Place the pasta mixture in a 7-inch (17.5cm) springform pan. Sprinkle the mozzarella and oregano over the top.

4. Place the pan in the fryer basket and cook until the mozzarella has melted and the edges are crispy, about 6 to 8 minutes.

5. Remove the pan from the fryer basket and allow the pasta bake to cool slightly before serving.

TIP | Roast vegetables such as broccoli, mushrooms, onion, eggplant, and zucchini in your air fryer. Place the vegetables in a large bowl, drizzle with a little olive oil, and sprinkle with a little kosher salt. Toss well to coat. Place the vegetables in the fryer basket and roast for 5 to 8 minutes.

NUTRITION PER 1 SERVING:

TOTAL FAT **4g** • SATURATED FAT **1g** • CHOLESTEROL **0mg** • SODIUM **295mg** • CARBS **52g**
DIETARY FIBERS **4g** • SUGARS **8g** • PROTEIN **9g**

Cauliflower Casserole
with Cashew Cream Sauce

Turn a pasta dish vegan with a cashew-based sauce. Roasted cauliflower helps displace some of the pasta and adds a veggie to the mix for a complete meal.

465 CALORIES PER SERVING

FRYER TEMP **400°F**

PREP TIME **20 mins**

COOK TIME **17 mins**

MAKES **4 servings** • SERVING SIZE **1 serving**

1 head of cauliflower, trimmed and chopped

¼ tsp kosher salt

1 tbsp olive oil

4 cups cooked elbow macaroni

½ cup shredded vegan mozzarella-style cheese (Daiya recommended)

red pepper flakes (optional)

FOR THE SAUCE

1 cup raw cashews

juice of 2 lemons

14oz (400g) canned coconut milk

2 tbsp nutritional yeast

¼ tsp garlic powder

1 tsp kosher salt

½ tsp freshly ground black pepper

1. To make the cream sauce, place the cashews in a medium bowl, cover with boiling water, and soak for 15 minutes. Drain the water and transfer the cashews to a blender. Add the lemon juice, coconut milk, nutritional yeast, garlic powder, salt, and pepper. Blend until smooth. Set aside.

2. Set the air fryer temp to 400°F. Spray 4 mini loaf pans with nonstick cooking spray. Set aside.

3. In a large bowl, combine the cauliflower, olive oil, and salt. Toss well to coat.

4. Place the cauliflower in the fryer basket and cook until slightly tender and the edges are golden brown, about 5 minutes. Clean out any crumbs from the fryer basket.

5. Transfer the cauliflower to a large bowl. Add the pasta and 1 cup of the sauce. Evenly divide the pasta mixture among the 4 pans. Sprinkle an equal amount of cheese over each mixture. (Refrigerate the remaining sauce for up to 5 days.)

6. Working in batches, place 2 pans in the fryer basket and cook until the cheese melts, about 5 to 6 minutes.

7. Remove the pans from the fryer basket. Allow the casseroles to cool slightly. Serve with the red pepper flakes (if using).

TIP Make the cashew cream ahead of time and store in the fridge. It tastes even better the next day. This recipe makes about 3 cups, so you'll have some left over.

NUTRITION PER 1 SERVING:

TOTAL FAT **20g** • SATURATED FAT **10g** • CHOLESTEROL **0mg** • SODIUM **370mg** • CARBS **61g** DIETARY FIBERS **5g** • SUGARS **6g** • PROTEIN **13g**

Lo Mein
with Brown Sugar Tofu

Early in my career, I set out to change minds about tofu—and this recipe is a great example. Toss with rice noodles and veggies for a complete meal.

523 CALORIES PER SERVING

FRYER TEMP **400°F**

PREP TIME **15 mins**

COOK TIME **12 mins**

MAKES **4 servings** • SERVING SIZE **1 serving**

14oz (400g) extra-firm tofu

1 tbsp cornstarch

1 tbsp plus 2 tsp light brown sugar

¼ tsp garlic powder

½ tsp kosher salt

2 tsp sesame oil

12oz (340g) rice noodles, cooked

2 tbsp reduced-sodium soy sauce

2 cups shredded carrots

1 cup diced cucumber

sriracha chili sauce

1. Set the air fryer temp to 400°F. Spray the fryer basket with nonstick cooking spray.

2. Dice the tofu and remove the liquid by gently pressing the tofu with paper towels.

3. In a medium bowl, combine the cornstarch, 1 tablespoon of brown sugar, garlic powder, and salt. Add the tofu and gently toss.

4. Add the tofu to the fryer basket and cook until golden and crispy, about 10 to 12 minutes. Remove the tofu from the fryer basket and set aside.

5. In a large nonstick saucepan on the stovetop over medium heat, warm the sesame oil. Add the noodles, soy sauce, and the remaining 2 teaspoons of brown sugar. Toss well and cook for 3 to 4 minutes.

6. Transfer the noodles to serving bowls. Top with the tofu, carrots, cucumber, and sriracha. Serve immediately.

TIP | Look for super-firm varieties of tofu. They require less draining.

NUTRITION PER 1 SERVING:

TOTAL FAT **11g** • SATURATED FAT **1.5g** • CHOLESTEROL **0mg** • SODIUM **610mg** • CARBS **83g**
DIETARY FIBERS **6g** • SUGARS **7g** • PROTEIN **20g**

Cashew Stir-Fry

This is hands down the easiest stir-fry you'll ever make. Plus, it has 20% of your daily iron needs per serving. The cashews add protein and healthy fats.

271 CALORIES PER SERVING

FRYER TEMP **400°F**

PREP TIME **10 mins**

COOK TIME **6 mins**

MAKES **4 servings** • SERVING SIZE **1 serving**

6 cups broccoli florets

1 red bell pepper, sliced

1 cup roasted cashews

1 tbsp canola or avocado oil

2 tsp rice vinegar

2 tsp agave nectar

2 tbsp reduced-sodium soy sauce

4 cups cooked brown rice

1. Set the air fryer temp to 400°F.

2. In a large bowl, combine the broccoli, bell pepper, and cashews. Add the oil and toss well to coat.

3. In a small bowl, whisk together the rice vinegar, agave, and soy sauce. Drizzle over the broccoli mixture.

4. Place everything in the fryer basket and cook for 6 minutes.

5. Transfer the stir-fry to a serving bowl and serve immediately with 1 cup of brown rice per serving.

TIP Some liquid will drip to the bottom of the basket. It's super flavorful, so be sure to pour this over the top before serving.

TIP Replace the soy sauce, agave, and vinegar mixture with 2 tablespoons of teriyaki sauce.

TIP You can also serve this dish with rice noodles.

NUTRITION PER 1 SERVING:

TOTAL FAT **17g** • SATURATED FAT **3g** • CHOLESTEROL **0mg** • SODIUM **361mg** • CARBS **25g** DIETARY FIBERS **5g** • SUGARS **8g** • PROTEIN **10g**

Lentil Empanadas
with THE Green Sauce

Traditionally made with butter, lard, and eggs, these flaky empanadas are 100% vegan. This recipe comes with a delectable green sauce—and it's addictive!

MAKES **8** • SERVING SIZE **2**

578 CALORIES PER SERVING

FRYER TEMP **400°F**

PREP TIME **30 mins**

COOK TIME **15 mins**

---

2 cups all-purpose flour, plus more

2 tsp kosher salt

8 tbsp coconut oil

iced water

1 cup cooked brown or green lentils

FOR THE SAUCE

1 medium avocado, diced

juice of 2 limes

2 bunches of fresh cilantro

1 jalapeño

2 tsp white vinegar

1 tbsp agave nectar

1 tsp kosher salt

¼ white onion

¾ cup water

1. Set the air fryer temp to 400°F.

2. In a blender, make the sauce by combining the ingredients. Blend until smooth. Transfer half the sauce to a serving bowl. Set aside. (Refrigerate the remaining sauce for up to 1 week.)

3. In a large bowl, combine the flour and salt. Add the coconut oil and use a pastry cutter or fork to incorporate the oil until distributed throughout the dry ingredients. Add iced water 1 tablespoon at a time and mix gently until a slightly sticky dough forms. (You should need about 7 to 8 tablespoons of water.) Form the dough into a disc and wrap in plastic wrap. Refrigerate for 1 hour.

4. Roll out the dough on a lightly floured surface and use a 4.5-inch (11.5cm) or 5-inch (12.5cm) ring mold to cut out 8 rounds.

5. Spoon an equal amount of the lentils in the center of each round. Gently fold the dough in half. Use a fork to crimp the edges closed.

6. Place the empanadas in the fryer basket and bake until golden brown, about 12 to 15 minutes. (You might need to do this in batches depending on the size of your air fryer.)

7. Transfer the empanadas to a platter and allow to cool slightly. Serve warm with the sauce.

TIP For best results, make the lentils in a pressure cooker. Sauté ½ cup of diced white onion and 1 chopped garlic clove with ½ teaspoon of kosher salt, ¼ teaspoon of freshly ground black pepper, and ½ teaspoon of ground cumin. Add 1 cup of dry green lentils, 2 cups of low-sodium vegetable broth, and a bay leaf. Cook on high pressure for 15 minutes. Allow the pressure to naturally release. This makes 3 cups.

NUTRITION PER 2 EMPANADAS:

TOTAL FAT **33g** • SATURATED FAT **24g** • CHOLESTEROL **0mg** • SODIUM **884mg** • CARBS **62g** DIETARY FIBERS **8g** • SUGARS **3g** • PROTEIN **12g**

Lentil Enchiladas

Lentils are an underappreciated plant-based food—an impressive protein source great for enchiladas begging to be drenched in tangy salsa verde.

MAKES **2** • SERVING SIZE **1**

342 CALORIES PER SERVING

FRYER TEMP **380°F**

PREP TIME **15 mins**

COOK TIME **10 mins**

2 cups cooked lentils

½ white onion, diced

3 tbsp chopped fresh cilantro

2 medium corn tortillas

½ cup salsa verde

½ cup shredded vegan Cheddar-style cheese

1. Set the air fryer temp to 380°F. Spray a baking dish with nonstick cooking spray.

2. In a medium bowl, combine the lentils, onion, and cilantro. Spoon an equal amount of the mixture into the center of each tortilla and roll them up. Place the tortillas in the dish and top with the salsa verde and cheese.

3. Place the dish in the fryer basket and cook until the edges are golden brown and the cheese has melted, about 10 minutes.

4. Remove the dish from the fryer basket and allow the enchiladas to cool slightly before serving.

TIP | To make the lentils, in a saucepan on the stovetop over high heat, combine 1 cup of lentils and 2 cups of low-sodium vegetable broth. Cook for 15 to 20 minutes.

NUTRITION PER 1 ENCHILADA:

TOTAL FAT **4g** • SATURATED FAT **1g** • CHOLESTEROL **0mg** • SODIUM **735mg** • CARBS **59g** DIETARY FIBERS **19g** • SUGARS **6g** • PROTEIN **21g**

Black Bean Quesadillas

This is an effortless lunch or dinner made with only four ingredients. Cut the quesadillas into wedges and serve as an appetizer with salsa and guacamole.

MAKES **8** • SERVING SIZE **2**

347 CALORIES PER SERVING

FRYER TEMP **380°F**

PREP TIME **10 mins**

COOK TIME **10 mins**

8 small flour tortillas (regular or whole grain)

1½ cups shredded vegan Cheddar-style or mozzarella-style cheese

1 cup canned black beans, drained and rinsed

½ cup chopped fresh cilantro

salsa

1. Set the air fryer temp to 380°F.

2. In the center of each tortilla, place an equal amount of cheese, beans, and cilantro. Fold the tortillas in half.

3. Working in batches, place 4 tortillas in the fryer basket and cook until the cheese has melted and the tops are golden and crispy, about 4 to 5 minutes.

4. Transfer the quesadillas to a platter and serve immediately with the salsa.

NUTRITION PER 2 QUESADILLAS:

TOTAL FAT **11g** • SATURATED FAT **6g** • CHOLESTEROL **0mg** • SODIUM **651mg** • CARBS **52g**
DIETARY FIBERS **5g** • SUGARS **1g** • PROTEIN **10g**

Tempeh & Walnut Tacos

Made from fermented soybeans, tempeh is not only a protein powerhouse, but it also has probiotics to help promote healthy digestion.

325 CALORIES PER SERVING

FRYER TEMP **330°F**

PREP TIME **10 mins**

COOK TIME **20 mins**

MAKES **8** • SERVING SIZE **2**

2 tsp canola oil

¼ tsp ground cumin

½ tsp kosher salt

½ tsp chili powder

8oz (225g) tempeh, diced

¾ cup chopped walnuts

⅓ cup mild salsa (Green Mountain Gringo recommended)

FOR SERVING

8 small corn tortillas, warmed

chopped romaine or iceberg lettuce

guacamole

1. Set the air fryer temp to 330°F.

2. In a medium bowl, combine the canola oil, cumin, salt, and chili powder. Add the tempeh and toss well to coat.

3. Place the tempeh in the fryer basket and cook for 10 minutes. Pause the machine to add the walnuts and shake the basket gently to toss them with the tempeh. Restart the machine and cook for 5 to 10 minutes more.

4. Transfer the tempeh and walnuts to a clean medium bowl. Add the salsa and toss well to coat.

5. Place the tempeh and walnut mixture in the tortillas. Serve with the lettuce and guacamole.

TIP | Prefer burritos? Roll this mixture into flour tortillas with cooked brown rice.

TIP | Mix up the texture by crumbling the tempeh instead.

NUTRITION PER 2 TACOS:

TOTAL FAT **15g** • SATURATED FAT **2g** • CHOLESTEROL **0mg** • SODIUM **380mg** • CARBS **38g** DIETARY FIBERS **8g** • SUGARS **3g** • PROTEIN **12g**

Spicy Jackfruit Tacos

Move over, pulled pork! These fiery tacos have all the flavor and texture you crave. The ingredients list features pantry staples you probably have on hand.

325 **CALORIES** PER SERVING

FRYER TEMP **400°F**

PREP TIME **10 mins**

COOK TIME **12 mins**

MAKES **8** • SERVING SIZE **2**

20oz (560g) canned jackfruit, rinsed, drained, and patted dry

1 tsp kosher salt

1 tsp smoked paprika

1 tsp chili powder

½ tsp ground cumin

1 tsp cornstarch

FOR SERVING

1 cup salsa

1 avocado, diced

1½ cups black beans

8 small corn tortillas, warmed

1. Set the air fryer temp to 400°F.

2. Roughly chop the jackfruit and discard any hard pieces. Place the jackfruit in a large bowl.

3. In a small bowl, combine the salt, paprika, chili powder, cumin, and cornstarch. Add this mixture to the jackfruit and toss well to coat. Place the jackfruit in a baking dish.

4. Place the dish in the fryer basket and cook until sizzling and crispy at the edges, about 12 minutes. Pause the machine halfway through to stir.

5. Remove the dish from the fryer basket and allow the jackfruit to cool slightly. Place an equal amount of jackfruit, salsa, avocado, and black beans on each tortilla. Serve immediately.

NUTRITION PER 2 TACOS:

TOTAL FAT **12g** • SATURATED FAT **2g** • CHOLESTEROL **0mg** • SODIUM **888mg** • CARBS **45g**
DIETARY FIBERS **14g** • SUGARS **5g** • PROTEIN **10g**

Cauliflower & Walnut Burrito Bowls

Cauliflower and walnuts create a magical texture combo. Experiment with the spices to turn up the heat. Use the filling for tacos, salads, and wraps.

524 CALORIES PER SERVING

FRYER TEMP **400°F**

PREP TIME **15 mins**

COOK TIME **15 mins**

MAKES **4** • SERVING SIZE **1**

2 cups cauliflower florets

½ cup walnuts

1 tbsp tomato paste

2 tsp olive oil

1 tsp kosher salt

1 garlic clove

2 tsp chili powder

1 cup canned black beans, rinsed and drained

4 cups cooked brown rice

1 avocado, diced

1 cup pico de gallo

1. Set the air fryer temp to 400°F.

2. Place the cauliflower, walnuts, tomato paste, olive oil, salt, garlic, and chili powder in a food processor. Pulse until finely chopped. Transfer the mixture to a baking dish.

3. Place the dish in the fryer basket and cook until crispy, about 12 to 15 minutes. Pause the machine frequently to stir the mixture.

4. Remove the dish from the fryer basket. Place an equal amount of the black beans, rice, cauliflower mixture, avocado, and pico de gallo into each of 4 bowls. Serve immediately.

NUTRITION PER 1 BOWL:

TOTAL FAT **26g** • SATURATED FAT **2g** • CHOLESTEROL **0mg** • SODIUM **610mg** • CARBS **61g** DIETARY FIBERS **11g** • SUGARS **2g** • PROTEIN **18g**

Sides

Falafel
with Tahini Sauce

346 CALORIES PER SERVING

FRYER TEMP **380°F**

PREP TIME **15 mins**

COOK TIME **12 mins**

Here's the absolutely best thing to do with chickpeas! Tuck these savory legumes into warmed pita bread with arugula and drench the falafel in tahini sauce.

MAKES **8 pieces** • SERVING SIZE **2 pieces**

15oz (420g) canned chickpeas, drained

¼ cup chickpea flour

2 garlic cloves

2 tbsp chopped red onion

¼ cup fresh parsley leaves, chopped

¾ tsp ground cumin

1 tsp kosher salt

3 tbsp olive oil

FOR THE SAUCE

¼ cup tahini

2 tbsp water

1 tbsp maple syrup

juice of ½ lemon

½ tsp kosher salt

1. Set the air fryer temp to 380°F.

2. In a food processor, combine the chickpeas, chickpea flour, garlic, onion, parsley, cumin, salt, and olive oil. Pulse until combined, being careful not to overmix. (You want the mixture to be combined but not smooth.) Divide the mixture into 8 equally sized patties and spray them on both sides with olive oil.

3. Place the patties in the fryer basket and cook until golden brown, about 10 to 12 minutes.

4. Make the tahini sauce in a small bowl by whisking together the ingredients until smooth.

5. Transfer the falafel to a platter. Cut the falafel into 8 pieces and serve immediately with the sauce.

TIP | No need to rinse the chickpeas—the canning liquid (also known as aquafaba) helps bind the ingredients together.

NUTRITION PER 2 PIECES:

TOTAL FAT **20g** • SATURATED FAT **3g** • CHOLESTEROL **0mg** • SODIUM **510mg** • CARBS **32g**
DIETARY FIBERS **9g** • SUGARS **8g** • PROTEIN **11g**

Rosemary Flatbread

Turn out the perfect batch of flatbread in minutes with the air fryer. You can easily double or triple this recipe to feed larger crowds.

183 CALORIES PER SERVING

FRYER TEMP **400°F**

PREP TIME **15 mins**

COOK TIME **10 mins**

MAKES **4 servings** • SERVING SIZE **1 serving**

2 tbsp olive oil

1 garlic clove, minced

2 tsp chopped fresh rosemary

1 tsp sea salt

8oz (225g) prepared pizza dough

1. Set the air fryer temp to 400°F.

2. In a small bowl, combine the olive oil, garlic, rosemary, and salt. Mix well. Divide the dough into 4 equally sized balls. On a lightly floured surface, press the dough into oblong shapes.

3. Working in batches, place 2 pieces of dough in the fryer basket. Spread an equal amount of the oil mixture over each piece of dough and cook for 5 minutes. Turn off the machine and allow the bread to rest in the fryer basket for 2 minutes.

4. Transfer the flatbread to a platter and allow to cool before serving.

TIP | Serve the flatbread with a soup, salad, or hummus and veggie platter.

NUTRITION PER 1 SERVING:

TOTAL FAT **7g** • SATURATED FAT **0g** • CHOLESTEROL **0mg** • SODIUM **320mg** • CARBS **24g**
DIETARY FIBERS **2g** • SUGARS **0g** • PROTEIN **4g**

Carrot Fries
with Lemon & Garlic Aioli

You've never had a fry like this! A quick trip in the air fryer helps the carrots further develop their natural sweetness. Plus, it gives them a hint of smoky char.

MAKES **32** • SERVING SIZE **8**

231 CALORIES PER SERVING

FRYER TEMP **330°F**

PREP TIME **10 mins**

COOK TIME **8 mins**

4 medium carrots, peeled and each cut into 8 sticks

2 tsp olive oil

1 tsp kosher salt

½ tsp freshly ground black pepper

FOR THE AIOLI

¼ cup aquafaba (from a 15oz [420g] can of chickpeas)

1 tsp Dijon mustard

1 small garlic clove, grated with a microplane

2 tsp freshly squeezed lemon juice

2 tsp lemon zest

¼ tsp kosher salt

¾ cup canola oil

1 tbsp chopped fresh dill

1. Set the air fryer temp to 330°F.

2. In a 16-ounce (450g) wide-mouth glass jar, make the aioli by using an immersion blender to combine the aquafaba, mustard, garlic, lemon juice and zest, and salt. With the blender going, slowly stream in the canola oil. Continue to blend as the mixture thickens. Taste for seasoning and adjust as needed.

3. Add the dill and mix with a spoon. Set aside. (Reserve half the aioli for another use.)

4. In a large bowl, combine the carrot sticks, olive oil, salt, and pepper. Toss well to coat.

5. Place the carrots in the fryer basket and cook until crisp-tender and they have tiny bits of charring on the edges, about 8 minutes.

6. Transfer the carrot fries to a platter and serve with the aioli.

TIP | If you don't have an immersion blender, use a countertop blender.

TIP | See pages 53, 55, and 126 for recipes that use chickpeas.

TIP | Refrigerate the remaining aioli for up to 5 days.

NUTRITION PER 8 FRIES + 2 TABLESPOONS AIOLI:

TOTAL FAT **20g** • SATURATED FAT **2g** CHOLESTEROL **0mg** • SODIUM **290mg** • CARBS **12g** DIETARY FIBERS **3g** • SUGARS **6g** • PROTEIN **1g**

Yucca Fries

Yucca is a starchy root veggie with endless culinary potential. Peel away the tough exterior to reveal a creamy white flesh that's sweeter than a potato's.

234 CALORIES PER SERVING

FRYER TEMP **350°F**

PREP TIME **5 mins**

COOK TIME **14 mins**

MAKES **4 servings** • SERVING SIZE **1 serving**

1¼lb (565g) yucca root, peeled

1 tbsp olive oil

½ tsp kosher salt

1. Set the air fryer temp to 350°F.

2. Cut the yucca into equally sized fries. In a large bowl, combine the fries, olive oil, and salt. Toss well to coat.

3. Place the fries in the fryer basket and cook until golden and crispy, about 10 to 14 minutes. Pause the machine halfway through to shake the basket.

4. Transfer the fries to a platter and serve immediately.

NUTRITION PER 1 SERVING:

TOTAL FAT **4g** • SATURATED FAT **1g** • CHOLESTEROL **0mg** • SODIUM **309mg** • CARBS **47g** DIETARY FIBERS **2g** • SUGARS **2g** • PROTEIN **2g**

Truffle Fries

With their deep, earthy flavor, truffles give air fryer fries a whole new identity. Leave the skins on the potatoes for an extra dose of minerals.

MAKES **4** • SERVING SIZE **1**

151 CALORIES
PER SERVING

FRYER TEMP **350°F**

PREP TIME **10 mins**

COOK TIME **18 mins**

1½lb (680g) russet potatoes

1 tbsp olive oil

¼ tsp kosher salt

1 tsp truffle salt

1. Set the air fryer temp to 350°F.

2. Cut the potatoes into equally sized fries. In a large bowl, combine the fries, olive oil, and kosher salt. Toss well to coat.

3. Place the fries in the fryer basket and cook until golden and crispy, about 15 to 18 minutes. Pause the machine halfway through to shake the basket.

4. Transfer the fries to a platter and season with the truffle salt before serving.

TIP | Look for truffle salt in specialty food shops. You don't need much— a little imparts huge flavor.

NUTRITION PER 1 SERVING:

TOTAL FAT **4g** • SATURATED FAT **1g** • CHOLESTEROL **0mg** • SODIUM **570mg** • CARBS **26g**
DIETARY FIBERS **4g** • SUGARS **1g** • PROTEIN **3g**

Polenta Fries

This whole grain take on fries is salty and crunchy on the outside and creamy on the inside. Dunk them in marinara sauce or serve them with chili.

MAKES **32** • SERVING SIZE **8**

230 CALORIES
PER SERVING

FRYER TEMP **400°F**

PREP TIME **5 mins**

COOK TIME **44 mins**

18oz (510g) prepared polenta

2 tsp olive oil

½ tsp kosher salt

¼ tsp freshly ground black pepper

2 cups marinara sauce

1. Set the air fryer temp to 400°F.

2. Cut the polenta in half and then into 32 fries that are ½ inch (1.25cm) thick.

3. In a large bowl, combine the polenta, olive oil, salt, and pepper. Toss well to coat.

4. Working in batches, place half the fries in the fryer basket and cook until golden and crispy, about 22 minutes.

5. Transfer the fries to a platter and serve with the marinara sauce.

TIP Prepared polenta is more compact and works best for this recipe. If you prefer to use leftover polenta that's been cooked and cooled, cut it into squares instead of sticks.

NUTRITION PER 8 FRIES:

TOTAL FAT **7g** · SATURATED FAT **2g** · CHOLESTEROL **0mg** · SODIUM **604mg** · CARBS **37g**
DIETARY FIBERS **4g** · SUGARS **11g** · PROTEIN **4g**

Crispy Brussels Sprouts

Deep-fried Brussels sprouts have become a trendy restaurant menu item. You can get the same crispy, caramelized goodness without the oily deep-frying.

80 CALORIES PER SERVING

FRYER TEMP **390°F**

PREP TIME **5 mins**

COOK TIME **16 mins**

MAKES **4 servings** • SERVING SIZE **1 serving**

1lb (450g) Brussels sprouts, trimmed and halved or quartered

1 tbsp olive oil

¾ tsp kosher salt

¾ tsp freshly ground black pepper

1. Set the air fryer temp to 390°F.

2. In a large bowl, combine the Brussels sprouts, olive oil, salt, and pepper. Toss well to coat.

3. Place the Brussels sprouts in the fryer basket and cook until caramelized and tender, about 16 minutes.

4. Transfer the Brussels sprouts to a serving bowl and allow to cool slightly. Serve warm.

TIP | For an extra burst of flavor, season with fresh lemon zest and more freshly ground black pepper right before serving.

NUTRITION PER 1 SERVING:

TOTAL FAT **4g** • SATURATED FAT **1g** • CHOLESTEROL **0mg** • SODIUM **466mg** • CARBS **10g** DIETARY FIBERS **4g** • SUGARS **2g** • PROTEIN **4g**

Stuffed Mushrooms

No one I know seems to tire of stuffed mushrooms. Double or triple this recipe for a crowd or make a bunch to serve with a salad for a main course.

219 CALORIES PER SERVING

FRYER TEMP **360°F**

PREP TIME **15 mins**

COOK TIME **10 mins**

MAKES **12** • SERVING SIZE **3**

8oz (225g) baby bella mushrooms

½ cup cooked brown rice

3 tbsp vegan cream cheese

2 tbsp chopped sun-dried tomatoes, packed in oil, drained

3 tbsp chopped fresh parsley

2 garlic cloves, finely chopped

4 tsp olive oil, divided, plus more

½ cup panko breadcrumbs, divided

kosher salt

freshly ground black pepper

1. Set the air fryer temp to 360°F.

2. Remove the stems from the mushrooms and roughly chop them. In a large bowl, combine the stems, rice, cream cheese, tomatoes, parsley, garlic, 2 teaspoons of olive oil, and ¼ cup of breadcrumbs.

3. Drizzle the insides of the mushroom caps with olive oil. Season with salt and pepper. Spoon the rice mixture into the mushrooms and sprinkle the remaining ¼ cup of breadcrumbs over the top. Drizzle the remaining 2 teaspoons of olive oil over the breadcrumbs.

4. Place the mushrooms in the fryer basket and cook until the tops are golden and crispy, about 10 minutes.

5. Transfer the mushrooms to a platter and allow to cool slightly before serving.

TIP | Stuff these mushrooms ahead of time and store them in the fridge. Pop them back in the air fryer right before serving.

NUTRITION PER 3 MUSHROOMS:

TOTAL FAT **11g** • SATURATED FAT **3g** • CHOLESTEROL **0mg** • SODIUM **215mg** • CARBS **25g**
DIETARY FIBERS **3g** • SUGARS **2g** • PROTEIN **5g**

Onion Rings

An order of fast-food onion rings has 700 calories and 40 grams of fat! Make them (a lot) lighter with aquafaba, the thick liquid from canned chickpeas.

MAKES **18** • SERVING SIZE **2**

177 CALORIES PER SERVING

FRYER TEMP **350°F**

PREP TIME **10 mins**

COOK TIME **20 mins**

1 large Vidalia onion

1 cup all-purpose flour

1 cup aquafaba (from a 15oz [420g] can of chickpeas)

2 cups panko breadcrumbs

1 tsp smoked paprika

1 tsp kosher salt

1. Set the air fryer temp to 350°F.

2. Slice the onion into 4 thick slices and separate into 18 total rings.

3. Place the flour, aquafaba, and breadcrumbs in three separate medium bowls. Season each bowl with an equal amount of paprika and salt.

4. Dredge the onion rings in the flour, then the aquafaba, followed by the breadcrumbs.

5. Working in batches, place 9 rings in the fryer basket and cook until golden brown and tender, about 10 minutes.

6. Transfer the onion rings to a plate and serve immediately.

TIP | See pages 53, 55, and 126 for recipes that use chickpeas.

NUTRITION PER 2 ONION RINGS:

TOTAL FAT **1g** • SATURATED FAT **0g** • CHOLESTEROL **0mg** • SODIUM **435mg** • CARBS **36g** DIETARY FIBERS **3g** • SUGARS **4g** • PROTEIN **5g**

Charred Corn Salsa

82 CALORIES PER SERVING

FRYER TEMP **400°F**

PREP TIME **10 mins**

COOK TIME **8 mins**

Yes, you *can* make salsa in the air fryer! Frozen corn is as nutritious as fresh, so enjoy this recipe all year. Jalapeños and cilantro add a perfect pop of green.

MAKES **3 cups** • SERVING SIZE **½ cup**

2 cups frozen corn kernels

½ cup finely chopped bell pepper (any color)

½ cup finely chopped red onion

1 garlic clove, finely chopped

1 tbsp olive oil

1 tsp kosher salt

3 tbsp chopped pickled jalapeños

½ cup roughly chopped fresh cilantro

tortilla chips

1. Set the air fryer temp to 400°F.

2. In a medium bowl, combine the corn, bell pepper, onion, garlic, olive oil, and salt.

3. Place the mixture in the fryer basket and cook until the veggies begin to char, about 6 to 8 minutes.

4. Transfer the salsa to a large bowl and mix in the jalapeños and cilantro. Serve immediately with the tortilla chips.

TIP | For a creamier version, mix in some diced avocado.

TIP | If you're concerned about small cut pieces falling through the basket, use a baking dish and stir the veggies once or twice during cooking.

NUTRITION PER ½ CUP:

TOTAL FAT **4g** • SATURATED FAT **1g** • CHOLESTEROL **0mg** • SODIUM **337mg** • CARBS **12g** DIETARY FIBERS **2g** • SUGARS **3g** • PROTEIN **2g**

Corn Fritters

These tasty treats are like hush puppies meet corn cakes. Broccoli adds a green veggie bonus and tahini helps bind everything together.

MAKES **6** • SERVING SIZE **2**

150 CALORIES PER SERVING

FRYER TEMP **390°F**

PREP TIME **10 mins**

COOK TIME **10 mins**

2 tbsp all-purpose flour

2 tbsp cornmeal

¼ tsp baking powder

½ tsp kosher salt

2 tbsp tahini

3 tbsp low-sodium vegetable broth

1 tsp chopped fresh thyme

1 tsp rice vinegar

1 cup corn kernels

½ cup finely chopped broccoli

THE Green Sauce (pg. 66) (optional)

1. Set the air fryer temp to 390°F.

2. In a medium bowl, whisk together the flour, cornmeal, baking powder, and salt. Add the tahini, vegetable broth, thyme, rice vinegar, corn, and broccoli. Mix well. (If the mixture seems too dry, add more broth 1 teaspoon at a time until a thick and sticky dough forms.)

3. With clean hands, divide the mixture into 6 equally sized patties. Spray the fryer basket and both sides of each fritter with nonstick cooking spray.

4. Place the fritters in the fryer basket and cook until puffed and slightly golden brown, about 10 minutes. Pause the machine halfway through to flip the fritters.

5. Transfer the fritters to a platter. Allow to cool for 3 to 5 minutes before serving with THE Green Sauce (if using).

TIP | These fritters are also mighty delish with salsa and guacamole.

NUTRITION PER 2 FRITTERS:

TOTAL FAT **6g** • SATURATED FAT **1g** • CHOLESTEROL **0mg** • SODIUM **362mg** • CARBS **21g**
DIETARY FIBERS **3g** • SUGARS **2g** • PROTEIN **5g**

Mini Eggplants
with Tahini Sauce

This unique spin on roasted eggplant boasts several heart-healthy Mediterranean flavors. The creamy sauce adds a dose of hunger-fighting healthy fats.

MAKES **4** • SERVING SIZE **2**

350 CALORIES PER SERVING

FRYER TEMP **300°F**

PREP TIME **10 mins**

COOK TIME **20 mins**

2 small eggplants

4 tsp olive oil

kosher salt

freshly ground black pepper

FOR THE SAUCE

¼ cup tahini

2 tsp agave nectar

¼ tsp ground cumin

1 tbsp freshly squeezed lemon juice

2 tbsp water

½ cup pomegranate seeds

2 tbsp chopped fresh mint

1. Set the air fryer temp to 300°F.

2. In a small bowl, make the tahini sauce by whisking together the tahini, agave, cumin, lemon juice, and water until smooth. (Add a few more drops of water if needed.) Set aside.

3. Cut the eggplants in half lengthwise. Use a paring knife to score the flesh lengthwise and across. (Be careful not to cut all the way through to the skin.)

4. Lay the eggplants on a flat surface and gently press to open. Drizzle olive oil over the flesh and season with salt and pepper.

5. Place the eggplants cut side up in the fryer basket and roast until tender and caramelized, about 20 minutes.

6. Transfer the eggplants to a serving platter. Drizzle the tahini sauce over the eggplants. Sprinkle the pomegranate seeds and mint around the platter. Serve immediately.

TIP | You can also do this with the smaller Japanese-style eggplant. Remember to reduce the cooking time accordingly.

NUTRITION PER 2 EGGPLANT HALVES:

TOTAL FAT **26g** • SATURATED FAT **3g** • CHOLESTEROL **0mg** • SODIUM **333mg** • CARBS **28g** DIETARY FIBERS **12g** • SUGARS **14g** • PROTEIN **8g**

Sesame Broccoli

This fast and fresh dish is perfect for stir-fry, salads, and noodle dishes. Cruciferous veggies like broccoli are known for their cancer-fighting properties.

57 CALORIES
PER SERVING

FRYER TEMP **400°F**

PREP TIME **2 mins**

COOK TIME **6 mins**

MAKES **6 servings** • SERVING SIZE **1 serving**

6 cups broccoli florets

1 tbsp sesame oil

1 tsp kosher salt

2 tsp sesame seeds, plus more

1. Set the air fryer temp to 400°F.

2. In a large bowl, combine the broccoli, sesame oil, and salt. Toss well to coat.

3. Place the broccoli in the fryer basket and cook for 5 minutes. Pause the machine and add the sesame seeds. Restart the machine and cook for 1 minute more.

4. Transfer the broccoli to a platter. Sprinkle more sesame seeds over the top before serving.

TIP | For an extra boost of flavor, toss the broccoli back in the bowl with the sesame oil.

NUTRITION PER 1 SERVING:

TOTAL FAT **3g** • SATURATED FAT **0g** • CHOLESTEROL **0mg** • SODIUM **418mg** • CARBS **6g**
DIETARY FIBERS **3g** • SUGARS **1g** • PROTEIN **3g**

Asparagus Tips

This veggie has folate (a B-vitamin that helps with cellular function) as well as vitamin K for healthy blood. Bite sizes make all the edges get extra crispy.

27 CALORIES PER SERVING

FRYER TEMP **380°F**

PREP TIME **2 mins**

COOK TIME **5 mins**

MAKES **2 servings** • SERVING SIZE **1 serving**

1 large bunch of asparagus

2 tsp olive oil

¼ tsp kosher salt

¼ tsp freshly ground black pepper

juice of ½ lemon

1. Set the air fryer temp to 380°F.

2. Remove and discard the tough ends of the asparagus stalks. Chop the stalks into 1-inch (2.5cm) pieces.

3. In a large bowl, combine the asparagus, olive oil, salt, and pepper. Toss well to coat.

4. Place the asparagus in the fryer basket and cook for 5 minutes or until they reach your desired doneness.

5. Transfer the asparagus to a serving bowl. Add the lemon juice and toss well to coat before serving.

NUTRITION PER 1 SERVING:

TOTAL FAT **0g** • SATURATED FAT **0g** • CHOLESTEROL **0mg** • SODIUM **293mg** • CARBS **5g** DIETARY FIBERS **3g** • SUGARS **3g** • PROTEIN **3g**

Hasselback Sweet Potatoes

Sweet potatoes feature healthy carbs, fiber, and lots of cell-protecting antioxidants—and this awesome presentation makes them even more craveable.

MAKES **4** • SERVING SIZE **1**

160 CALORIES PER SERVING

FRYER TEMP **300°F**

PREP TIME **3 mins**

COOK TIME **20 mins**

4 medium Hasselback sweet potatoes

4 tsp olive oil

1 tsp kosher salt

½ tsp freshly ground black pepper

1. Set the air fryer temp to 300°F.

2. Use a fork to poke a few holes in each sweet potato. Microwave the sweet potatoes for 3 minutes.

3. Use a sharp knife to make a series of ⅛-inch (3mm) slices along the top of each potato. Go only two-thirds of the way down so the potato remains in one piece.

4. Drizzle each potato with 1 teaspoon of olive oil. Season each with ½ teaspoon of salt and ¼ teaspoon of pepper.

5. Place the sweet potatoes in the fryer basket and bake until tender and the tops are crispy, about 20 minutes.

6. Transfer the potatoes to a platter and allow to cool slightly before serving.

TIP | To ensure even cooking, use sweet potatoes that are similar in size.

NUTRITION PER 1 SWEET POTATO:

TOTAL FAT **4g** · SATURATED FAT **1g** · CHOLESTEROL **0mg** · SODIUM **432mg** · CARBS **33g** DIETARY FIBERS **4g** · SUGARS **7g** · PROTEIN **2g**

Rosemary Potato Wedges

Crunchy edges, the fluffiest insides, and fresh rosemary make these wedges even more delicious. Chop up leftovers for the tastiest home fries.

MAKES **36** • SERVING SIZE **9**

176 CALORIES PER SERVING

FRYER TEMP **400°F**

PREP TIME **10 mins**

COOK TIME **22 mins**

2 large russet potatoes, unpeeled

2 tbsp finely chopped fresh rosemary

1 tsp sea salt

1 tbsp olive oil

1. Set the air fryer temp to 400°F.

2. Cut the potatoes in half and then into wedges. (You should have about 36 total pieces.) Place the wedges in a large bowl.

3. In a small bowl, combine the rosemary and salt. Drizzle the olive oil over the potatoes and add half the salt mixture. Toss well to coat.

4. Place the potatoes in the fryer basket and cook until golden and crispy, about 20 to 22 minutes. Pause the machine halfway through to shake the basket.

5. Transfer the wedges to a platter and allow to cool slightly. Season with the remaining rosemary salt before serving.

TIP | Add lemon zest to the rosemary salt to sprinkle over the potatoes right as they come out of the air fryer.

NUTRITION PER 9 WEDGES:

TOTAL FAT **4g** • SATURATED FAT **1g** • CHOLESTEROL **0mg** • SODIUM **9mg** • CARBS **33g**
DIETARY FIBERS **2g** • SUGARS **1g** • PROTEIN **4g**

Butternut Squash Gratin

Sink your fork into tender butternut squash bathed in a thick and creamy (but creamless) sauce. This is cozy comfort food—but lighter in calories and fat.

167 CALORIES PER SERVING

FRYER TEMP **400°F**

PREP TIME **10 mins**

COOK TIME **20 mins**

MAKES **2 servings** • SERVING SIZE **1 serving**

1 tbsp vegan butter (Earth Balance recommended)

¼ cup finely chopped yellow onion

1 garlic clove, minced

½ tsp kosher salt

1 tsp dried thyme leaves

1 tbsp all-purpose flour

½ cup low-sodium vegetable broth

½ cup unsweetened almond milk

10oz (285g) fresh butternut squash, thinly sliced or spiralized

1. Set the air fryer temp to 400°F. Spray a baking pan with nonstick cooking spray. Set aside.

2. In a medium saucepan on the stovetop over medium heat, melt the butter. Add the onion, garlic, salt, and thyme. Sauté for 3 to 4 minutes. Sprinkle in the flour and cook for 2 minutes more.

3. Stir in the vegetable broth and almond milk. Simmer until thickened, about 2 to 3 minutes.

4. Turn off the heat and gently stir in the squash. Transfer the mixture to the pan.

5. Place the pan in the fryer basket and bake until bubbly and golden brown on the top, about 20 minutes.

6. Remove the pan from the fryer basket and allow the gratin to cool slightly before serving.

NUTRITION PER 1 SERVING:

TOTAL FAT **8g** • SATURATED FAT **1g** • CHOLESTEROL **0mg** • SODIUM **534mg** • CARBS **22g**
DIETARY FIBERS **4g** • SUGARS **4g** • PROTEIN **4g**

Snacks & Salads

Avocado Egg Rolls

Egg rolls and air fryers make a dynamic duo. Complement this crispy, crunchy, high-protein snack with a salad for a supreme meal.

290 CALORIES PER SERVING

FRYER TEMP **300°F**

PREP TIME **10 mins**

COOK TIME **6 mins**

MAKES **8** • SERVING SIZE **2**

1 large avocado, diced

½ cup black beans, rinsed and drained

2 tbsp salsa, plus more

¼ cup corn kernels

2 tbsp chopped fresh cilantro

8 egg roll wrappers

1. Set the air fryer temp to 300°F.

2. In a medium bowl, combine the avocado, black beans, salsa, corn, and cilantro.

3. Place 2 tablespoons of the mixture in the center of each egg roll wrapper. Fold a corner over the filling, tuck in the sides, and roll up from the bottom to the top. Wet the top with water to help secure the seal. Spray the egg rolls with canola oil.

4. Place the egg rolls in the fryer basket. Cook until golden brown, about 5 to 6 minutes, turning once halfway through.

5. Transfer the egg rolls to a platter and serve immediately with more salsa.

TIP | You can use any veggies you have on hand for these egg rolls.

NUTRITION PER 2 EGG ROLLS:

TOTAL FAT **8g** • SATURATED FAT **2g** • CHOLESTEROL **0mg** • SODIUM **309mg** • CARBS **45g**
DIETARY FIBERS **9g** • SUGARS **3g** • PROTEIN **12g**

Panko-Crusted Avocado Wedges

Never pass up an opportunity to cook an avocado—it's surprisingly delicious. Creamy flesh gets a flash (air) fry to become encrusted with breadcrumbs.

117 CALORIES PER SERVING

FRYER TEMP **390°F**

PREP TIME **15 mins**

COOK TIME **12 mins**

MAKES **16** • SERVING SIZE **2**

2 medium ripe avocados, halved and pitted

½ cup aquafaba (from a 15oz [420g] can of chickpeas)

1½ cups panko breadcrumbs

½ tsp kosher salt

1. Set the air fryer temp to 390°F. Spray the fryer basket with nonstick cooking spray.

2. Slice each avocado into 8 wedges. Place the aquafaba and breadcrumbs in separate medium bowls. Dip the wedges in the aquafaba and then in the breadcrumbs.

3. Working in batches, place 8 wedges in the fryer basket and cook until golden, about 5 to 6 minutes.

4. Transfer the wedges to a platter and sprinkle the salt over the top. Serve immediately.

TIP | For some spiciness, add a few dashes of hot sauce to the aquafaba.

NUTRITION PER 2 WEDGES:

TOTAL FAT **7g** • SATURATED FAT **1g** • CHOLESTEROL **0mg** • SODIUM **165mg** • CARBS **12g**
DIETARY FIBERS **4g** • SUGARS **0g** • PROTEIN **3g**

Blooming Onion
with Yum Yum Sauce

157 CALORIES PER SERVING

FRYER TEMP **380°F**

PREP TIME **10 mins**

COOK TIME **22 mins**

This copycat recipe gets a healthy, less oily upgrade with the air fryer. Aquafaba allows the crunchy topping to adhere to the tender onion petals.

MAKES **4 servings** • SERVING SIZE **1 serving**

½ cup aquafaba (from a 15oz [420g] can of chickpeas)

½ cup all-purpose flour

¼ tsp kosher salt

½ cup seasoned breadcrumbs

1 large Vidalia onion

FOR THE SAUCE

2 tbsp vegan mayonnaise

2 tbsp dairy-free plain yogurt

2 tbsp ketchup

1 to 2 tsp sriracha chili sauce

1. Set the air fryer temp to 380°F.

2. Place the aquafaba in a medium shallow bowl. In a separate medium bowl, combine the flour, salt, and breadcrumbs.

3. Slice the top off the onion and turn it over to rest on a flat surface. Cut several slits around the entire onion, then turn it over and gently spread out the petals. Dip the onion in the aquafaba and then in the flour mixture. Sprinkle the flour mixture in between the petals and shake off any excess. Spray the onion with canola oil.

4. Place the onion in the fryer basket and cook until golden brown, about 20 to 22 minutes.

5. In a small bowl, make the yum yum sauce by whisking together the ingredients until smooth.

6. Transfer the blooming onion to a platter and serve immediately with the sauce.

NUTRITION PER 1 SERVING:

TOTAL FAT **3g** • SATURATED FAT **0g** • CHOLESTEROL **0mg** • SODIUM **317mg** • CARBS **28g**
DIETARY FIBERS **2g** • SUGARS **5g** • PROTEIN **4g**

Beet Chips
with Creamy Dill Sauce

This earthy, sweet root veggie contains potassium, folate, and fiber, plus blood pressure–lowering compounds—a great superfood for making chips.

MAKES **32** • SERVING SIZE **8**

267 CALORIES PER SERVING

FRYER TEMP **315°F**

PREP TIME **10 mins**

COOK TIME **24 mins**

4 medium red and golden beets, trimmed and peeled

sea salt

FOR THE SAUCE

1 cup raw cashews, soaked in water for at least 2 hours or overnight

juice of ½ lemon

1 cup water

1 tsp kosher salt

¼ tsp garlic powder

¼ cup chopped fresh dill

1. Set the air fryer temp to 315°F.

2. In a blender, make the dill sauce by combining the cashews, lemon juice, and water. Blend until smooth. Add the kosher salt, garlic powder, and dill. Blend for a few seconds more. Place the sauce in a serving bowl and set aside.

3. Use a mandoline slicer to cut the beets into ⅛-inch (3 mm) slices. Spray the beets with canola oil.

4. Working in batches, place half the beet slices in the fryer basket in a single layer. Cook until crispy and a little wrinkled, about 10 to 12 minutes. Pause the machine halfway through to shake the basket.

5. Transfer the beets to a platter and allow to cool. Sprinkle the sea salt over the chips. Serve with 1 cup of the dill sauce. (Refrigerate the remaining sauce for up to 3 days.)

TIP | Don't have time to soak the cashews for several hours? Place the cashews in a bowl and cover with boiling water, cover with plastic wrap, and let soak for 15 minutes.

TIP | Use a crinkle-cut blade if you have one to give the chips fun ruffles.

NUTRITION PER 8 CHIPS:

TOTAL FAT **16g** • SATURATED FAT **3g** • CHOLESTEROL **0mg** • SODIUM **413mg** • CARBS **27g** DIETARY FIBERS **6g** • SUGARS **13g** • PROTEIN **8g**

Spicy Kale Chips

Kale chips are still one of the hottest food trends around. Making these chips in an air fryer makes them easier to cook, more affordable, and crispier.

61 CALORIES PER SERVING

FRYER TEMP **370°F**

PREP TIME **10 mins**

COOK TIME **10 mins**

MAKES **4 servings** • SERVING SIZE **1 serving**

5 cups packed kale leaves, stems removed

2 tsp canola oil

½ tsp chili powder

½ tsp kosher salt

1. Set the air fryer temp to 370°F.

2. In a large bowl, combine the kale and canola oil. Add the chili powder and salt. Gently massage the leaves with the spices.

3. Working in batches, place half the kale in the fryer basket and cook until crispy, about 4 to 5 minutes. Pause the machine halfway through to shake the basket.

4. Transfer the chips to a platter and allow to cool before serving.

TIP | For a smokier edge, use some chipotle chili powder.

NUTRITION PER 1 SERVING:

TOTAL FAT **3g** • SATURATED FAT **0g** • CHOLESTEROL **0mg** • SODIUM **175mg** • CARBS **8g**
DIETARY FIBERS **2g** • SUGARS **1g** • PROTEIN **3g**

Sweet Potato Chips
with Olive Tapenade

Crisp sweet potatoes and a briny olive mixture will check all your flavor boxes. Basically, just make these sweet and savory chips every weekend!

MAKES **32** · SERVING SIZE **8**

153 CALORIES PER SERVING

FRYER TEMP **350°F**

PREP TIME **10 mins**

COOK TIME **24 mins**

2 medium sweet potatoes

chopped fresh parsley

FOR THE TAPENADE

1 cup pitted green or black olives

¼ cup sun-dried tomatoes, packed in oil, drained and chopped

2 tbsp chopped fresh parsley

1 tbsp olive oil

½ tsp kosher salt

½ tsp freshly ground black pepper

1. Set the air fryer temp to 350°F.

2. In a food processor, make the tapenade by combining the ingredients. Pulse until well combined. Transfer the tapenade to a medium bowl and set aside.

3. Use a mandoline slicer to cut the sweet potatoes into ⅛-inch (3 mm) slices.

4. Working in batches, place half the potato slices in a single layer in the fryer basket. Spray with canola oil. Cook until crispy and a little wrinkled, about 10 to 12 minutes. Pause the machine halfway through to shake the basket.

5. Transfer the sweet potato chips to a platter to cool. Top with the tapenade and sprinkle the parsley over the top before serving.

NUTRITION PER 8 CHIPS:

TOTAL FAT **7g** · SATURATED FAT **1g** · CHOLESTEROL **0mg** · SODIUM **327mg** · CARBS **22g**
DIETARY FIBERS **3g** · SUGARS **4g** · PROTEIN **2g**

Tomato & Garlic Bruschetta

A quick toss in the air fryer brings out the nutty and sweet qualities of the aromatic garlic and elevates this classic recipe to all-star appetizer status.

157 CALORIES PER SERVING

FRYER TEMP **400°F**

PREP TIME **10 mins**

COOK TIME **11 mins**

MAKES **16 slices** • SERVING SIZE **2 slices**

6 large garlic cloves, peeled

1 tbsp olive oil

1 tsp kosher salt, divided, plus more

1 pint (300g) cherry tomatoes, quartered

¼ cup chopped fresh basil

2 tbsp balsamic vinegar, plus more

1 baguette

1. Set the air fryer temp to 400°F.

2. Place the garlic in a baking dish. Add the olive oil and ½ teaspoon of salt. Toss well to coat.

3. Place the dish in the fryer basket and cook until tender and golden brown, about 5 minutes.

4. Remove the garlic from the fryer basket and roughly chop. In a large bowl, combine the garlic, tomatoes, basil, balsamic vinegar, and the remaining ½ teaspoon of salt. Mix gently.

5. Cut the baguette into 16 equally sized slices.

6. Working in batches, place 8 baguette slices in the fryer basket and cook until toasted, about 2 to 3 minutes.

7. Transfer the slices to a platter. Top with the garlic and tomato mixture. Season with more salt and balsamic vinegar if desired.

TIP | This recipe is perfect for tomatoes fresh from the garden in summer or with jarred sun-dried tomatoes when fresh aren't in season.

TIP | For a "cheesy" version, top the toasted bread with shredded vegan mozzarella-style cheese (Daiya recommended) and return to the air fryer to melt. Then add the tomato mixture.

NUTRITION PER 2 BAGUETTE SLICES:

TOTAL FAT **3g** • SATURATED FAT **1g** • CHOLESTEROL **0mg** • SODIUM **486mg** • CARBS **28g**
DIETARY FIBERS **2g** • SUGARS **3g** • PROTEIN **6g**

Mini Toasted Cheese Sandwiches

Garlic bread meets grilled cheese in these delightful and oh-so-savory sandwiches. As an added bonus, they have spinach and apple tucked inside.

MAKES **12** • SERVING SIZE **3**

444 CALORIES PER SERVING

FRYER TEMP **370°F**

PREP TIME **15 mins**

COOK TIME **14 mins**

2 tbsp olive oil

1 garlic clove, minced

1 package of 12 dinner rolls

8 slices vegan Cheddar-style cheese

2 cups baby spinach

1 Granny Smith apple, cored and thinly sliced

1. Set the air fryer temp to 370°F.

2. In a small bowl, combine the olive oil and garlic. Set aside.

3. The rolls come connected as one large piece. Cut this piece in half and slice the 2 halves horizontally.

4. Working in batches, place 1 bottom half of rolls in the fryer basket and top with half the cheese, spinach, and apple slices. Place 1 top half of rolls on top. Brush half the olive oil mixture over the top. Cook until golden brown on top and the cheese has melted, about 5 to 7 minutes.

5. Transfer the rolls to a platter to cool slightly. Cut the 2 roll halves into 12 sandwiches before serving.

TIP | For an extra boost of (low-calorie) flavor, spread the bread with Dijon mustard before cooking.

TIP | Use a serrated knife to cut the bread into the 12 sliders.

NUTRITION PER 3 SANDWICHES:

TOTAL FAT **18g** • SATURATED FAT **4g** • CHOLESTEROL **0mg** • SODIUM **543mg** • CARBS **59g** DIETARY FIBERS **4.5g** • SUGARS **10g** • PROTEIN 11G

Potato Skins

These tater skins are a super-healthy side dish. Fill them with your favorite vegetables and experiment with different types of vegan cheeses.

MAKES **8** • SERVING SIZE **1**

150 CALORIES PER SERVING

FRYER TEMP **390°F**

PREP TIME **15 mins**

COOK TIME **37 mins**

4 medium russet potatoes, scrubbed

2 tbsp olive oil

1 tsp kosher salt

½ tsp freshly ground black pepper

1½ cups chopped broccoli

½ cup shredded vegan Cheddar-style cheese

dairy-free yogurt or sour cream (optional)

1. Set the air fryer temp to 390°F. Spray the fryer basket with nonstick cooking spray.

2. Poke the potatoes with a fork. Place them in the fryer basket and cook until tender, about 25 minutes.

3. Remove the potatoes from the fryer basket to cool. Cut them in half lengthwise and scoop out some of the flesh. Brush the insides with olive oil and season with salt and pepper. Top each potato skin with broccoli and cheese.

4. Working in batches, place 2 potatoes in the fryer basket and cook until the broccoli is crisp-tender and the cheese has melted, about 5 to 6 minutes.

5. Transfer the potato skins to a platter and serve immediately with the yogurt (if using).

TIP | Make a dairy-free sour "cream" in a blender by combining 1 cup of cashews, ½ cup of vegan yogurt, 1 teaspoon of cider vinegar, and ½ teaspoon of kosher salt. Blend until smooth.

TIP | Time-saving hack: Precook the potatoes in the microwave for 7 to 10 minutes. Then slice, fill, and crisp up in the air fryer.

NUTRITION PER 1 POTATO SKIN:

TOTAL FAT **7g** • SATURATED FAT **3g** • CHOLESTEROL **0mg** • SODIUM **403mg** • CARBS **21g**
DIETARY FIBERS **4g** • SUGARS **2g** • PROTEIN **3g**

Buffalo Cauliflower Bites

I've spent years figuring out the perfect combo of spicy and crunchy—and this is it! This dish also makes a surprisingly amazing taco filling.

MAKES **3 cups** • SERVING SIZE **¾ cup**

137 CALORIES PER SERVING

FRYER TEMP **360°F**

PREP TIME **10 mins**

COOK TIME **19 mins**

2 tbsp vegan butter (Earth Balance recommended), melted

2 tbsp hot sauce (Frank's RedHot recommended)

1 large head of cauliflower, trimmed and chopped

1 cup panko breadcrumbs

1. Set the air fryer temp to 360°F.

2. In a large bowl, combine the butter and hot sauce. Add the cauliflower and toss well to coat.

3. Place the cauliflower in the fryer basket and cook until slightly golden brown, about 12 minutes.

4. Remove the cauliflower from the fryer basket. In a clean large bowl, combine the cauliflower and breadcrumbs. Toss gently to coat.

5. Place the cauliflower in the fryer basket and cook until the breadcrumbs are golden brown, about 5 to 7 minutes.

6. Transfer the cauliflower to a platter and serve immediately.

TIP | These don't need a sauce, but they're definitely yummy dipped in the **Lemon & Garlic Aioli** (pg. 78).

NUTRITION PER ¾ CUP:

TOTAL FAT **4g** • SATURATED FAT **1g** • CHOLESTEROL **0mg** • SODIUM **406mg** • CARBS **21g**
DIETARY FIBERS **5g** • SUGARS **4g** • PROTEIN **6g**

"Mozzarella" Sticks

Going dairy-free doesn't mean no more fried cheese sticks. Soy-based cheese works best because the high-protein content helps hold the sticks together.

MAKES **10** • SERVING SIZE **2**

175 CALORIES
PER SERVING

FRYER TEMP **380°F**

PREP TIME **15 mins**

COOK TIME **8 mins**

10oz (285g) block vegan mozzarella-style cheese (Follow Your Heart recommended)

½ cup aquafaba (from a 15oz [420g] can of chickpeas)

2 cups seasoned breadcrumbs

½ tsp kosher salt

marinara sauce

1. Set the air fryer temp to 380°F. Spray the fryer basket with nonstick cooking spray.

2. Cut the mozzarella into 10 sticks. Place the aquafaba and breadcrumbs in separate medium bowls. Dip the cheese in the aquafaba and then in the breadcrumbs.

3. Place the cheese in the fryer basket and cook until golden, about 7 to 8 minutes.

4. Transfer the cheese sticks to a platter and season with salt. Allow them to cool slightly before serving with the marinara sauce.

NUTRITION PER 2 STICKS:

TOTAL FAT **14g** • SATURATED FAT **0g** • CHOLESTEROL **0mg** • SODIUM **417mg** • CARBS **20g**
DIETARY FIBERS **0g** • SUGARS **0g** • PROTEIN **4g**

Corn Chips
with Homemade "Queso"

Whip up a quick batch of chips and queso for your next movie night. Tortillas made from a blend of corn and wheat flour have an amazing crunch.

MAKES **48** · SERVING SIZE **12**

224 CALORIES PER SERVING

FRYER TEMP **400°F**

PREP TIME **10 mins**

COOK TIME **8 mins**

8 medium corn and wheat flour tortillas

sea salt

FOR THE QUESO

1 cup **Cashew Cream Sauce** (pg. 63)

2 tbsp water

½ cup salsa

2 tsp nutritional yeast

1 tsp ground turmeric

1. Set the air fryer temp to 400°F.

2. In a small saucepan on the stovetop over medium-low heat, make the queso by combining the ingredients. Stir until everything's well incorporated, about 4 to 5 minutes. Keep warm.

3. Cut the tortillas in half and cut each half into 3 triangles.

4. Working in batches, add half the triangles to the fryer basket and spray with canola oil. Cook until golden, about 3 to 4 minutes.

5. Transfer the tortillas to a baking sheet and spread them in an even layer. (They'll crisp up as they cool.) Season with the salt and serve immediately with the queso.

TIP | You can use corn tortillas for a gluten-free version.

NUTRITION PER 12 CHIPS + ⅓ CUP QUESO:

TOTAL FAT **15g** · SATURATED FAT **8g** · CHOLESTEROL **0mg** · SODIUM **402mg** · CARBS **20g**
DIETARY FIBERS **3g** · SUGARS **3g** · PROTEIN **5g**

Citrus Salad
with Toasted Rosemary Almonds

310 CALORIES PER SERVING

FRYER TEMP **320°F**

PREP TIME **15 mins**

COOK TIME **6 mins**

Almonds have heart-healthy fats and other essential nutrients, like fiber, protein, and vitamin E. Pile these crunchy nuts on this bright and citrusy salad.

MAKES **6 servings** • SERVING SIZE **1 serving**

2 tsp gluten-free tamari or reduced-sodium soy sauce

1 tbsp finely chopped fresh rosemary

pinch of garlic powder

6oz (170g) raw almonds

2 large oranges, sectioned

12 cups mixed greens

FOR THE DRESSING

¼ cup extra virgin olive oil

juice of ½ lemon

1 tbsp rice vinegar

1 tsp Dijon mustard

½ small shallot, finely chopped

2 tsp agave nectar

¼ tsp kosher salt

¼ tsp freshly ground black pepper

1. Set the air fryer temp to 320°F.

2. In a medium bowl, combine the tamari, rosemary, garlic powder, and almonds. Toss well to coat.

3. Place the almonds in the fryer basket and cook for 5 to 6 minutes. Pause the machine halfway through to toss and to make sure no small pieces are burning.

4. Transfer the almonds to a sheet pan and allow to cool completely. Set aside.

5. In a large bowl, make the dressing by whisking together the ingredients. Taste for seasoning and adjust as needed.

6. In a separate large bowl, combine the orange segments, the mixed greens, and half the almonds.

7. Drizzle the dressing over the top and toss well to coat. Top with the remaining almonds and serve immediately.

TIP | Don't have a shallot? Add a whole peeled garlic clove to the dressing to infuse it with flavor and to avoid munching on raw chunks.

TIP | Toasted and cooled almonds can be stored in an airtight container for up to 4 days.

NUTRITION PER 1 SERVING:

TOTAL FAT **22g** • SATURATED FAT **2g** • CHOLESTEROL **0mg** • SODIUM **349mg** • CARBS **22g**
DIETARY FIBERS **7g** • SUGARS **9g** • PROTEIN **9g**

Beet Salad

Don't count out salads for your air fryer. This combo of fresh veggies, homemade dressing, and air-fried goodies makes for a show-shopping salad.

491 CALORIES PER SERVING

FRYER TEMP **400°F**

PREP TIME **10 mins**

COOK TIME **10 mins**

MAKES **4 servings** • SERVING SIZE **1 serving**

2 medium beets, peeled and diced

1 tbsp olive oil, divided

½ tsp kosher salt, divided

8 cups mixed greens

Crispy Garlic Chickpeas (pg. 126)

1 cup grated carrots

1 cup crumbly vegan havarti-style or Monterey Jack–style cheese

FOR THE DRESSING

2 tbsp olive oil

1 tbsp balsamic vinegar

½ tsp kosher salt

½ tsp freshly ground black pepper

1. Set the air fryer temp to 400°F.

2. In a large bowl, make the dressing by whisking together the ingredients. Set aside.

3. In a separate large bowl, combine the beets, olive oil, and salt. Toss well to coat.

4. Place the beets in the fryer basket and cook until tender, about 8 to 10 minutes.

5. Transfer the beets to a platter and allow to cool for 10 minutes. Place the greens on top of the dressing. Add the beets, chickpeas, carrots, and cheese. Toss well to coat and serve immediately.

TIP | Beets and orange are a beautiful pairing. Add some fresh orange juice and zest to the dressing if desired.

TIP | Make this salad ahead of time. Assemble and toss with the dressing just before serving.

NUTRITION PER 1 SERVING:

TOTAL FAT **18g** • SATURATED FAT **4g** • CHOLESTEROL **0mg** • SODIUM **882mg** • CARBS **69g**
DIETARY FIBERS **20g** • SUGARS **16g** • PROTEIN **15g**

Kale Caesar Salad
with Tangy Garlic Dressing

This salad boasts 6 grams of fiber and 13 grams of protein—great for a super-satisfying lunch. The secret to the dressing is piquant miso paste.

374 CALORIES PER SERVING

FRYER TEMP **390°F**

PREP TIME **10 mins**

COOK TIME **3 mins**

MAKES **2 servings** • SERVING SIZE **1 serving**

1½ cups cubed whole grain bread

2 tsp olive oil

6 cups chopped kale

⅓ cup shredded vegan Parmesan-style cheese

FOR THE DRESSING

2 tbsp vegan mayonnaise

1 tbsp olive oil

juice of 1 lemon

2 tsp white miso paste

1 garlic clove, minced

½ tsp Dijon mustard

½ tsp kosher salt

½ tsp freshly ground black pepper

1. Set the air fryer temp to 390°F.

2. In a medium bowl, make the dressing by whisking together the ingredients. Taste for seasoning and adjust as needed. Set aside.

3. In a large bowl, combine the bread and olive oil.

4. Place the bread in the fryer basket and cook until toasted, about 2 to 3 minutes. Remove the croutons from the fryer basket and set aside to cool slightly.

5. In a large bowl, place the kale and Parmesan. Top with the croutons. Drizzle the dressing over the top. Toss well to coat. Divide the salad into 2 bowls before serving.

TIP | To make the crunchiest croutons, use day-old bread.

NUTRITION PER 1 SERVING:

TOTAL FAT **20g** • SATURATED FAT **3g** • CHOLESTEROL **0mg** • SODIUM **610mg** • CARBS **38g** DIETARY FIBERS **6g** • SUGARS **3g** • PROTEIN **13g**

Veggie Burger & Jícama Tacos

Tuck any taco filling into thin slices of this root vegetable for a quick and easy weeknight dinner— the best low-carb taco replacement you've ever had.

275 CALORIES PER SERVING

FRYER TEMP **380°F**

PREP TIME **15 mins**

COOK TIME **13 mins**

MAKES **8** • SERVING SIZE **2**

1 red onion, sliced

1 bell pepper (any color), sliced

4 premade plant-based burgers (Dr. Praeger's recommended)

1 large jícama, thinly sliced into rounds

FOR SERVING (OPTIONAL)

diced avocados

pickled jalapeños

bell peppers (any color)

chopped romaine or iceberg lettuce

vegan cheese

Tempeh & Walnut Tacos
(pg. 71)

Buffalo Cauliflower Bites
(pg. 112)

1. Set the air fryer temp to 380°F.

2. Place the onion and pepper slices in the fryer basket and cook for 2 to 3 minutes.

3. Pause the machine to place the burgers on top of the vegetables. Restart the machine and cook until the veggies are tender and the burgers are heated through, about 8 to 10 minutes.

4. Transfer the veggies and burgers to a cutting board. Allow to cool slightly and then roughly chop. Scoop an equal amount of the mixture into 8 jícama shells. Add desired toppings before serving.

NUTRITION PER 2 TACOS:

TOTAL FAT **4g** • SATURATED FAT **0g** • CHOLESTEROL **0mg** • SODIUM **478mg** • CARBS **48g** DIETARY FIBERS **22g** • SUGARS **9g** • PROTEIN **17g**

Veggie Burger Salad
with Everything Croutons

This springtime-inspired salad makes the perfect light lunch. The best part is crispy homemade croutons spiced to taste like an everything bagel.

435 CALORIES PER SERVING

FRYER TEMP **390°F**

PREP TIME **10 mins**

COOK TIME **11 mins**

MAKES **4 servings** • SERVING SIZE **1 serving**

4 veggie burgers

2 cups cubed whole grain bread

2 tsp olive oil

2 tsp Everything Bagel Seasoning

8 cups baby spinach

1 cup sliced strawberries

2 cups diced cucumber

½ cup favorite salad dressing

1. Set the air fryer temp to 390°F.

2. Place the burgers in the fryer basket and cook for 4 minutes per side. Remove the burgers from the fryer basket and roughly chop. Set aside.

3. Place the bread in a large bowl and drizzle with the olive oil.

4. Place the cubes in the fryer basket and cook until toasted, about 2 to 3 minutes.

5. Transfer the croutons to a clean large bowl and add the seasoning. Toss well to coat.

6. In a separate large bowl, combine the spinach, strawberries, and cucumber. Add the croutons, burgers, and dressing. Toss well to coat.

7. Divide the salad into 4 bowls before serving.

TIP | To make a quick dressing, in a medium bowl, whisk together 1 cup of dairy-free yogurt, 1 tablespoon of Dijon mustard, ¼ teaspoon of kosher salt, ⅛ teaspoon of freshly ground black pepper, and 1 tablespoon of agave nectar.

NUTRITION PER 1 SERVING:

TOTAL FAT **28g** • SATURATED FAT **3g** • CHOLESTEROL **0mg** • SODIUM **656mg** • CARBS **20g**
DIETARY FIBERS **6g** • SUGARS **4g** • PROTEIN 23G

Apple & Spinach Salad
with Whole Grain Croutons

381 CALORIES PER SERVING

FRYER TEMP **390°F**

PREP TIME **10 mins**

COOK TIME **3 mins**

This easy everyday salad feels extra special topped with air-fried croutons. Apples, spinach, and walnuts have plenty of anti-inflammatory properties.

MAKES **4 servings** • SERVING SIZE **1 serving**

2 cups cubed whole grain bread

2 tsp olive oil

8 cups baby spinach

1 medium Gala apple, chopped

15oz (420g) canned chickpeas, rinsed and drained

½ cup toasted walnuts

½ cup favorite salad dressing

1. Set the air fryer temp to 390°F.

2. Place the bread in a large bowl and drizzle with the olive oil.

3. Place the cubes in the fryer basket and cook until toasted, about 2 to 3 minutes.

4. Transfer the croutons to a platter and allow to cool slightly. In a large bowl, combine the spinach, apple, chickpeas, and walnuts. Top with the croutons and dressing. Toss well to coat.

5. Divide the salad into 4 bowls before serving.

TIP | For a quick dressing, whisk together ¼ cup of extra virgin olive oil, 2 tablespoons of balsamic vinegar, 2 teaspoons of Dijon mustard, 2 teaspoons of maple syrup, 1 garlic clove minced, ¼ teaspoon of kosher salt, and ⅛ teaspoon of freshly ground black pepper.

TIP | Place the walnuts in the air fryer for 1 to 2 minutes at 390°F to get them toasty.

NUTRITION PER 1 SERVING:

TOTAL FAT **24g** • SATURATED FAT **3g** • CHOLESTEROL **0mg** • SODIUM **319mg** • CARBS **33g**
DIETARY FIBERS **9g** • SUGARS **8g** • PROTEIN **13g**

Roasted Veggie Soup

This soup is the answer for lunch or dinner on any chilly day. Parboiling the potatoes before air frying makes for an even cooking time for all the veggies.

157 CALORIES PER SERVING

FRYER TEMP **400°F**

PREP TIME **10 mins**

COOK TIME **7 mins**

MAKES **1 quart** • SERVING SIZE **1 cup**

8 small red potatoes, halved

2 cups chopped cauliflower

1 cup chopped broccoli

1 tbsp olive oil

1 tsp kosher salt

1 tsp freshly ground black pepper

3 cups low-sodium vegetable broth

whole grain crackers or **Crispy Garlic Chickpeas** (pg. 126)

1. Set the air fryer temp to 400°F.

2. Place the potatoes in a microwave-safe bowl and cover with water. Microwave the potatoes until tender, about 4 to 5 minutes.

3. Drain the water and place the potatoes in a large bowl. Add the cauliflower, broccoli, olive oil, salt, and pepper. Toss well to coat.

4. Place the vegetables in the fryer basket and roast until slightly tender and the edges are golden brown, about 5 to 7 minutes.

5. Transfer the vegetables to a medium saucepan on the stovetop over medium heat. Add the vegetable broth. Reduce the heat to low and bring to a simmer. Use an immersion or countertop blender to blend until smooth. Taste for seasoning and adjust as needed.

6. Transfer the soup to bowls and serve immediately with the whole grain crackers.

TIP | For a creamier soup, add 2 tablespoons of the **Cashew Cream Sauce** (pg. 63) before blending.

TIP | Leave the skin on the potatoes—they have several nutrients you don't want to peel away.

NUTRITION PER 1 CUP:

TOTAL FAT **4g** • SATURATED FAT **1g** • CHOLESTEROL **0mg** • SODIUM **435mg** • CARBS **29g**
DIETARY FIBERS **4g** • SUGARS **4g** • PROTEIN **4g**

Crispy Garlic Chickpeas

Nothing fights an afternoon energy slump like this munchable high-protein snack. They're also a healthier replacement for croutons on a salad.

MAKES **6 servings** • SERVING SIZE **1 serving**

69 CALORIES
PER SERVING

FRYER TEMP **390°F**

PREP TIME **5 mins**

COOK TIME **15 mins**

15oz (420g) canned chickpeas, drained and rinsed

1 tbsp olive oil

1 tsp kosher salt

1 tsp freshly ground black pepper

½ tsp garlic powder

½ tsp dried thyme leaves

1. Set the air fryer temp to 390°F.

2. In a medium bowl, combine the chickpeas, olive oil, salt, pepper, and garlic powder. Toss well to coat.

3. Place the chickpeas in the fryer basket and cook until crisped or as desired, about 13 to 15 minutes. Pause the machine 2 or 3 times to shake the basket.

4. Transfer the chickpeas to a serving bowl. Add the thyme and toss well to coat. Allow the chickpeas to cool before serving.

TIP | Store the chickpeas in an airtight container for up to 5 days.

TIP | For a sweet take, toss the chickpeas with 1 tablespoon of olive oil, ½ teaspoon of ground cinnamon, and 2 teaspoons of light brown sugar.

TIP | For extra flavor, season with fresh lemon zest before serving.

NUTRITION PER 1 SERVING:

TOTAL FAT **3g** • SATURATED FAT **1g** • CHOLESTEROL **0mg** • SODIUM **207mg** • CARBS **9g** DIETARY FIBERS **2g** • SUGARS **0g** • PROTEIN **2g**

Tempeh Jerky

Nutty tempeh takes on a whole new identity when turned into jerky. Use the lowest possible heat setting to cook down this faux jerky low and slow.

69 CALORIES
PER SERVING

FRYER TEMP **180°F**

PREP TIME **10 mins**

COOK TIME **45 mins**

MAKES **24 pieces** • SERVING SIZE **3 pieces**

2 tbsp gluten-free tamari or reduced-sodium soy sauce

1 tsp sesame oil

1 tbsp rice vinegar

1 tbsp ketchup

2 tsp molasses

8oz (225g) tempeh, sliced into 24 thin slices

1. In a shallow dish, whisk together the tamari, sesame oil, rice vinegar, ketchup, and molasses. Add the tempeh and marinate for at least 30 minutes or up to overnight in the fridge.

2. Set the air fryer temp to 180°F. Spray the fryer basket with nonstick cooking spray.

3. Pat the tempeh dry with paper towels. Place in the fryer basket and cook until brown and slightly crispy, about 45 minutes.

4. Transfer the jerky to a platter and allow to cool completely before serving.

TIP | Store the jerky in an airtight container for up to 4 days.

TIP | For some extra smoky flavor, add a few drops of liquid smoke.

NUTRITION PER 3 PIECES:

TOTAL FAT **3g** • SATURATED FAT **1g** • CHOLESTEROL **0mg** • SODIUM **127mg** • CARBS **5g** DIETARY FIBERS **0g** • SUGARS **1g** • PROTEIN **5g**

Mini Mushroom Pizzas

In this recipe, the mushroom *is* the pizza. Slather a portobello with marinara sauce and vegan cheese, then send it into the air fryer for a quick toast.

179 CALORIES PER SERVING

FRYER TEMP **380°F**

PREP TIME **10 mins**

COOK TIME **20 mins**

MAKES **4** • SERVING SIZE **1**

4 portobello mushrooms

½ cup marinara sauce, divided

1 cup shredded vegan mozzarella-style cheese (Daiya recommended)

1 tsp dried oregano

1. Set the air fryer temp to 380°F.

2. Remove the stems from the mushrooms and use a spoon to scoop out the gills. Use a paper towel to remove any dirt or debris on the top. Place the mushrooms stem side up on a cutting board and spread 2 tablespoons of marinara sauce over each mushroom. Sprinkle an equal amount of cheese and oregano over the top of each mushroom.

3. Working in batches, place 2 mushrooms in the fryer basket and cook until the cheese has melted and the edges of the mushrooms are crispy, about 8 to 10 minutes.

4. Transfer the mushroom pizzas to plates and allow to cool slightly before serving.

TIP | Make these pizzas ahead of time and freeze them before baking. They can go right from the freezer to the air fryer—just increase the cook time by about 5 minutes.

NUTRITION PER 1 PIZZA:

TOTAL FAT **6g** • SATURATED FAT **1g** • CHOLESTEROL **0mg** • SODIUM **507mg** • CARBS **27g**
DIETARY FIBERS **4g** • SUGARS **8g** • PROTEIN **7g**

Kale Salad
with Spicy Miso Dressing

Inspired by my favorite noodle house, this salad checks all the flavor boxes: savory, sweet, crunchy, creamy, and umami.

344 CALORIES PER SERVING

FRYER TEMP **370°F**

PREP TIME **15 mins**

COOK TIME **2 mins**

MAKES **4 servings** • SERVING SIZE **1 serving**

12 cups chopped kale, stems removed, divided

2 tsp olive oil

1 avocado, diced

⅓ cup golden raisins

FOR THE DRESSING

2 tbsp canola oil

1 tsp sesame oil

1 tbsp rice vinegar

1 tsp Dijon mustard

1 tsp reduced-sodium soy sauce or gluten-free tamari

2 tsp white miso

1 tsp agave nectar or maple syrup

½ tsp freshly grated ginger

1. Set the air fryer temp to 370°F.

2. In a large bowl, combine 4 cups of kale and the olive oil.

3. Place the kale in the fryer basket and cook for 2 minutes.

4. To make the dressing, in the same large bowl (leaving the olive oil in it), whisk together the ingredients.

5. Transfer the cooked kale to the dressing bowl. Add the avocado, raisins, and the remaining 8 cups of raw kale. Toss well to coat. Serve immediately.

NUTRITION PER 1 SERVING:

TOTAL FAT **20g** • SATURATED FAT **3g** • CHOLESTEROL **0mg** • SODIUM **287mg** • CARBS **37g** DIETARY FIBERS **7g** • SUGARS **9g** • PROTEIN **8g**

Quinoa-Stuffed Peppers

502 CALORIES PER SERVING

FRYER TEMP **360°F**

PREP TIME **15 mins**

COOK TIME **20 mins**

These red peppers contain a savory mixture of beans, mushrooms, quinoa, and marinara. I often make this with whatever veggies I have available.

MAKES **4 halves** • SERVING SIZE **2 halves**

½ cup chopped mushrooms

1 cup cooked quinoa

½ cup cannellini beans or chickpeas, rinsed and drained

½ cup low-sodium vegetable broth

¼ cup marinara sauce

2 tsp chopped fresh thyme

2 medium red bell peppers

1 cup shredded vegan mozzarella-style cheese (Daiya recommended)

1. Set the air fryer temp to 360°F. Spray the fryer basket with nonstick cooking spray.

2. In a large bowl, combine the mushrooms, quinoa, cannellini beans, vegetable broth, marinara sauce, and thyme.

3. Cut each pepper in half lengthwise and remove the seeds. Fill each pepper with an equal amount of the quinoa mixture. Sprinkle an equal amount of the mozzarella over the top of each pepper.

4. Place the peppers in the fryer basket and cook until tender and the tops are crispy and golden brown, about 20 minutes.

5. Transfer the peppers to a platter and allow to cool slightly before serving.

TIP | If you don't like the cheese on the crispier side, wait until the last 5 minutes of cooking to add it to the peppers.

NUTRITION PER 2 HALVES:

TOTAL FAT **11g** • SATURATED FAT **3g** • CHOLESTEROL **0mg** • SODIUM **578mg** • CARBS **83g**
DIETARY FIBERS **12g** • SUGARS **10g** • PROTEIN **20g**

Desserts

S'mores

Who needs a campfire when you've got an air fryer? Get perfectly toasted marshmallows and ooey, gooey chocolate every time.

235 **CALORIES** PER SERVING

FRYER TEMP **350°F**

PREP TIME **5 mins**

COOK TIME **3 mins**

MAKES **4** • SERVING SIZE **1**

4 squares vegan dark chocolate

4 large vegan marshmallows

4 full graham crackers, halved

1. Set the air fryer temp to 350°F.

2. Place 1 chocolate square and 1 marshmallow on 1 cracker half. Repeat this step with 3 more cracker halves.

3. Place the s'mores in the fryer basket and cook until the marshmallow is puffed and golden, about 2 to 3 minutes.

4. Transfer the s'mores to a platter. Top each with a remaining cracker half and serve immediately.

TIP | Add fruit! Slip some thinly sliced strawberry, apple, or banana into your s'mores before or after cooking.

NUTRITION PER 1 S'MORE:

TOTAL FAT **12g** • SATURATED FAT **0g** • CHOLESTEROL **0mg** • SODIUM **101mg** • CARBS **34g**
DIETARY FIBERS **3g** • SUGARS **17g** • PROTEIN **3g**

Pear Clafoutis

Don't let the fancy French name fool you. This rustic dessert of pancake meets cake is one of the easiest fruity delights you could ever make.

196 **CALORIES** PER SERVING

FRYER TEMP **340°F**

PREP TIME **10 mins**

COOK TIME **25 mins**

MAKES **4 servings** • SERVING SIZE **1 serving**

2 cups medium pears, finely chopped

juice of ½ lemon

½ cup granulated sugar, divided

¼ cup whole wheat pastry flour

1 tsp baking powder

⅛ tsp kosher salt

½ tsp ground cinnamon

½ cup unsweetened soy milk

1 tbsp canola oil

1. Set the air fryer temp to 340°F.

2. In a baking dish, combine the pears, lemon juice, and 2 tablespoons of sugar.

3. In a large bowl, whisk together the pastry flour, baking powder, salt, and cinnamon. Add the soy milk, canola oil, and the remaining 6 tablespoons of sugar. Mix until a smooth batter forms. Pour the batter over the pears.

4. Place the dish in the fryer basket and bake until the cake is puffed and golden, about 20 to 25 minutes.

5. Remove the dish from the fryer basket and allow the cake to cool slightly before serving.

NUTRITION PER 1 SERVING:

TOTAL FAT **4g** • SATURATED FAT **0g** • CHOLESTEROL **0mg** • SODIUM **90mg** • CARBS **40g**

DIETARY FIBERS **3g** • SUGARS **30g** • PROTEIN **2g**

Blackberry Shortcake
with Orange-Spiked Cream

Shortcake-style desserts are one of my favorite things to make in the air fryer. The high heat and circulating air make the flakiest biscuits ever!

400 CALORIES PER SERVING

FRYER TEMP **320°F**

PREP TIME **20 mins**

COOK TIME **12 mins**

MAKES **4 slices** · SERVING SIZE **1 slice**

1 cup all-purpose flour

2 tbsp granulated sugar

1½ tsp baking powder

⅛ tsp kosher salt

2 tbsp coconut oil

¼ cup unsweetened soy milk

2 cups fresh blackberries

FOR THE CREAM

14oz (400g) canned coconut milk, refrigerated overnight

1½ tbsp powdered sugar

2 tsp orange zest

1. Set the air fryer temp to 320°F.

2. To make the cream, turn over the can of coconut milk and open the bottom. Drain the liquid (reserve for another use) and scoop the remaining solids (about ¾ cup) into the bowl of a stand mixer fitted with the whisk attachment. Add the powdered sugar and orange zest and whisk until fluffy, about 2 to 3 minutes. Set aside. (You'll have about ¼ cup of cream left over. Refrigerate for up to 3 days.)

3. In a large bowl, whisk together the flour, granulated sugar, baking powder, and salt. Add the coconut oil and use a pastry cutter to work the oil into the flour until distributed throughout the dry ingredients.

4. Add the soy milk and use clean hands to gently mix. Be careful not to overmix. Gently press the dough into a baking dish.

5. Place the dish in the fryer basket and bake until the edges are golden, about 12 minutes.

6. Remove the dish from the fryer basket and allow the shortcake to cool for 10 minutes.

7. Transfer the shortcake to a serving platter and cut into 4 slices. Top each slice with 2 tablespoons of cream and an equal amount of the blackberries before serving.

TIP | Flavor the biscuits without adding any calories with a sprinkle of ground cinnamon or a few teaspoons of orange zest before baking.

NUTRITION PER 1 SLICE:

TOTAL FAT **15g** · SATURATED FAT **12g** · CHOLESTEROL **0mg** · SODIUM **130mg** · CARBS **63g**

DIETARY FIBERS **4g** · SUGARS **33g** · PROTEIN **5g**

Blueberry Crisp

173 **CALORIES** PER SERVING

FRYER TEMP **370°F**

PREP TIME **10 mins**

COOK TIME **17 mins**

I love making this simple yet impressive dessert—a wonderful way to enjoy any fresh berry or seasonal fruit. Serve with a scoop of dairy-free ice cream.

MAKES **4 servings** • SERVING SIZE **1 serving**

2 cups fresh blueberries

juice of ½ orange

1 tbsp maple syrup

2 tsp cornstarch

1 tbsp vegan butter (Earth Balance recommended)

½ cup rolled oats

¼ cup almond flour

½ tsp ground cinnamon

2 tbsp coconut sugar or granulated sugar

pinch of kosher salt

1. Set the air fryer temp to 370°F.

2. In a baking dish, combine the blueberries, orange juice, maple syrup, and cornstarch. Mix well.

3. In a large bowl, combine the butter, oats, almond flour, cinnamon, sugar, and salt. Use clean hands to mix until a soft, crumbly dough forms. Evenly sprinkle the dough over the blueberries.

4. Place the dish in the fryer basket and bake until the topping is crispy and the berries are thick and bubbly, about 15 to 17 minutes.

5. Remove the dish from the fryer basket and allow the crisp to cool for at least 10 minutes before serving.

TIP | Use certified gluten-free oats to make this recipe celiac-friendly.

NUTRITION PER 1 SERVING:

TOTAL FAT **8g** • SATURATED FAT **6g** • CHOLESTEROL **0mg** • SODIUM **84mg** • CARBS **38g** DIETARY FIBERS **1g** • SUGARS **13g** • PROTEIN **4g**

Peach Parfaits
with Walnuts

This parfait is decadent without the guilt. The air fryer cooks peaches tender, and the crunchy and sweet topping is the ideal flavor and texture balance.

MAKES **8 servings** • SERVING SIZE **2 servings**

189 CALORIES
PER SERVING

FRYER TEMP **350°F**

PREP TIME **10 mins**

COOK TIME **12 mins**

3 tbsp light brown sugar

⅓ cup chopped walnuts

¼ tsp sea salt

4 peaches, halved and pits removed

6oz (170g) dairy-free plain yogurt

1. Set the air fryer temp to 350°F.

2. In a small bowl, combine the brown sugar, walnuts, and salt. Mix well.

3. Place the peaches in the fryer basket. Evenly sprinkle the walnut mixture over the peaches. Cook until the peaches are slightly tender and the sugar has begun to caramelize, about 10 to 12 minutes.

4. Transfer the peaches to a platter to cool slightly. Top with the yogurt before serving.

TIP | Use a soy-based yogurt to add protein to this recipe.

NUTRITION PER 2 SERVINGS:

TOTAL FAT **7g** • SATURATED FAT **0g** • CHOLESTEROL **0mg** • SODIUM **123mg** • CARBS **22g** DIETARY FIBERS **4g** • SUGARS **20g** • PROTEIN **5g**

Profiteroles

Traditionally made with eggs, cream, and butter, this vegan version of these finger-licking cream puffs is unbelievably close to the real thing.

MAKES **10** • SERVING SIZE **2**

2 tbsp vegan butter (Earth Balance recommended)

¼ cup unsweetened soy milk

1 tsp pure vanilla extract

1 tbsp maple syrup

3 tbsp liquid egg substitute (JUST Egg recommended)

1 cup all-purpose flour

1 tsp baking powder

¼ tsp kosher salt

FOR THE CREAM

14oz (400g) canned coconut milk, refrigerated overnight

1½ tbsp powdered sugar

FOR THE DRIZZLE

¼ cup vegan chocolate chips

½ tsp coconut oil

1. Set the air fryer temp to 375°F. Spray the fryer basket with nonstick cooking spray.

2. In a medium saucepan on the stovetop over medium-low heat, melt the butter. Add the soy milk, vanilla extract, maple syrup, and egg. Whisk to combine. Add the flour, baking powder, and salt. Mix well with a wooden spoon until a sticky dough forms. Turn off the heat and allow to cool for 2 minutes. Add the warm dough to a piping bag with a wide tip.

3. Pipe the dough directly into the fryer basket, forming 10 mounds the size of golf balls. Dampen your finger with water and gently press down the top of each mound to prevent burning. Cook until puffed and golden brown, about 10 minutes.

4. Transfer the profiteroles to a platter and allow to cool.

5. To make the cream, turn over the can of coconut milk and open the bottom. Drain the liquid (reserve for another use) and scoop the remaining solids (about ¾ cup) into the bowl of a stand mixer fitted with the whisk attachment. Add the powdered sugar and whisk until fluffy, about 2 to 3 minutes. Set aside.

6. Place the chocolate chips and coconut oil in a microwave-safe dish. Microwave for 60 to 90 seconds. Stir until combined and glossy.

7. Use a serrated knife to slice each profiterole in half and fill with a heaping spoonful of cream. (You'll have about half the cream left over. Refrigerate for up to 3 days for another use.) Drizzle the profiteroles with the chocolate sauce and serve immediately.

NUTRITION PER 2 PROFITEROLES:

TOTAL FAT **9g** • SATURATED FAT **6g** • CHOLESTEROL **0mg** • SODIUM **181mg** • CARBS **38g** DIETARY FIBER**s 1g** • SUGARS **19g** • PROTEIN **4g**

Cinnamon Twists

Looking for a great way to use leftover pie dough?
Don't have the motivation to make cookies? These
are a stellar—and deliciously sweet—substitute.

90 CALORIES PER SERVING

FRYER TEMP **330°F**

PREP TIME **10 mins**

COOK TIME **12 mins**

MAKES **20** • SERVING SIZE **2**

2 cups all-purpose flour,
  plus more

½ tsp kosher salt

½ cup canola oil

5 to 8 tbsp cold water

¼ cup granulated sugar

1½ tsp ground cinnamon

1. Set the air fryer temp to 330°F.

2. In a medium bowl, combine the flour and salt.

3. In a separate medium bowl, combine the oil and 5 to 6 tablespoons of the water. Make a well in the center of the flour mixture and pour in the oil mixture. Mix with a fork until just combined. Add 1 to 2 more tablespoons of water as needed.

4. In a small bowl, combine the sugar and cinnamon.

5. On a lightly floured surface, roll out the dough into a 10-inch (25cm) round. Cut the dough into 10 strips and then cut each strip in half. Sprinkle the sugar and cinnamon mixture on both sides and gently twist each strip.

6. Working in batches, place 10 twists in the fryer basket and cook until golden brown, about 5 to 6 minutes.

7. Transfer the cinnamon twists to a platter and allow to cool slightly before serving.

NUTRITION PER 2 TWISTS:

TOTAL FAT **4g** · SATURATED FAT **1g** · CHOLESTEROL **0mg** · SODIUM **98mg** · CARBS **12g**
DIETARY FIBERS **0g** · SUGARS **7g** · PROTEIN **1g**

Chocolate & Banana Egg Rolls

Fried desserts are all the rage but clearly not the healthiest—and many aren't vegan. This recipe is so delicious, adults and kiddos alike will beg for it.

243 CALORIES PER SERVING

FRYER TEMP **370°F**

PREP TIME **10 mins**

COOK TIME **6 mins**

MAKES **4** • SERVING SIZE **1**

4 egg roll wrappers

4 tbsp vegan chocolate and hazelnut spread or nut butter

2 small bananas, halved

powdered sugar

1. Set the air fryer temp to 370°F.

2. Place 1 wrapper on a flat surface, with the pointed end facing up. Spread the butter in the middle and top with half a banana. Fold in the sides over the filling and then roll up from bottom to top. Repeat this step with the remaining wrappers and filling. Spray the egg rolls with canola oil.

3. Place the egg rolls in the fryer basket and cook until golden brown, about 5 to 6 minutes, turning once halfway through.

4. Transfer the egg rolls to a platter and allow to cool for at least 10 minutes. Dust with the powdered sugar before serving.

NUTRITION PER 1 ROLL:

TOTAL FAT **6g** • SATURATED FAT **2g** • CHOLESTEROL **0mg** • SODIUM **191mg** • CARBS **40g**
DIETARY FIBERS **4g** • SUGARS **11g** • PROTEIN **12g**

Lemon Bars

OMG, do I love lemon bars! You can also make this tangy, sweet treat with any kind of citrus. Adding lemon zest to the filling offers even more lemony goodness.

283 CALORIES PER SERVING

FRYER TEMP **350°F**

PREP TIME **25 mins**

COOK TIME **22 mins**

MAKES **6** • SERVING SIZE **1**

4 tbsp coconut oil, melted

¼ tsp plus 1 pinch of kosher salt

1 tsp pure vanilla extract

½ cup plus 3 tbsp granulated sugar

½ cup plus 2 tbsp all-purpose flour

¼ cup freshly squeezed lemon juice

zest of 1 lemon

½ cup canned coconut cream

4 tbsp cornstarch

powdered sugar

1. Set the air fryer temp to 350°F.

2. In a medium bowl, combine the coconut oil, ¼ teaspoon of salt, vanilla extract, and 3 tablespoons of sugar. Mix in the flour until a soft dough forms. Transfer the mixture to a baking dish and gently press the dough to cover the bottom.

3. Place the dish in the fryer basket and bake until golden, about 10 minutes. Remove the crust from the fryer basket and set aside to cool slightly.

4. In a medium saucepan on the stovetop over medium heat, combine the lemon juice and zest, coconut cream, the pinch of kosher salt, and the remaining ½ cup of sugar,. Whisk in the cornstarch and cook until thickened, about 5 minutes. Pour the lemon mixture over the crust.

5. Place the dish in the fryer basket and cook until the mixture is bubbly and almost completely set, about 10 to 12 minutes.

6. Remove the dish from the fryer basket and set aside to cool completely. Transfer the dish to the refrigerator for at least 4 hours. Dust with the powdered sugar and slice into 6 bars before serving.

TIP | To make the bars extra yellow, add a sprinkle of ground turmeric or a drop of yellow food coloring.

NUTRITION PER 1 BAR:

TOTAL FAT **16g** • SATURATED FAT **14g** • CHOLESTEROL **0mg** • SODIUM **1mg** • CARBS **35g** DIETARY FIBERS **1g** • SUGARS **23g** • PROTEIN **2g**

Peanut Butter Cookies

Make a batch of fresh-baked cookies in 10 minutes! These are crispy on the edges, chewy in the centers, and bursting with peanut butter flavor.

MAKES **18** • SERVING SIZE **1**

126 CALORIES PER SERVING

FRYER TEMP **330°F**

PREP TIME **10 mins**

COOK TIME **10 mins**

1 tbsp ground flaxseed

3 tbsp water

1 cup creamy peanut butter (Skippy recommended)

¾ cup light brown sugar

⅔ cup all-purpose flour

1 tsp baking soda

½ tsp kosher salt

1. In a small bowl, combine the flaxseed and water in a small bowl. Mix well and set aside for 5 minutes.

2. In a large bowl, combine the peanut butter and brown sugar. Add the flaxseed mixture, flour, baking soda, and salt. Mix until a soft dough forms. Refrigerate the dough for at least 20 minutes.

3. Set the air fryer temp to 330°F. Spray the fryer basket with nonstick cooking spray.

4. Use a small scoop or tablespoon to roll the dough into 18 equally sized balls. Use a fork to press a diagonal hash mark into each ball.

5. Working in batches, place 9 balls in the fryer basket and cook until slightly golden, about 5 minutes.

6. Transfer the cookies to a wire rack to cool before serving.

TIP | Craving a chocolate and peanut butter combo? Add ⅓ cup of vegan mini chocolate chips to the dough.

TIP | Like a little crunch? Sprinkle the tops of the cookies with sparkling sugar before baking.

NUTRITION PER 1 COOKIE:

TOTAL FAT **6g** • SATURATED FAT **2g** • CHOLESTEROL **0mg** • SODIUM **205mg** • CARBS **12g**
DIETARY FIBERS **1g** • SUGARS **7g** • PROTEIN **4g**

Vanilla Confetti Cake
with Buttercream Frosting

Many store-bought cake mixes are vegan, so with a few simple swaps, you can bake it without eggs—and using the air fryer!

MAKES **4 slices** • SERVING SIZE **1 slice**

339 CALORIES PER SERVING

FRYER TEMP **310°F**

PREP TIME **15 mins**

COOK TIME **30 mins**

1½ cups vegan vanilla cake mix

¾ cup unsweetened applesauce

2 tbsp canola oil

¼ cup water

2 tbsp colored sprinkles

FOR THE FROSTING

3 tbsp vegan butter (Earth Balance recommended)

1 cup powdered sugar

½ tsp pure vanilla extract

pinch of kosher salt

1 to 2 tbsp unsweetened soy milk

1. Set the air fryer temp to 310°F. Spray a baking dish with nonstick cooking spray.

2. In a large bowl, whisk together the cake mix, applesauce, canola oil, and water. Fold in the sprinkles. Place the mixture in the dish.

3. Place the dish in the fryer basket and bake until the top is golden and a toothpick comes out clean from the center, about 30 minutes.

4. In a medium bowl, make the frosting by beating together the butter, powdered sugar, vanilla extract, and salt until well combined. Continue to mix while adding 1 to 2 tablespoons of soy milk to reach the desired consistency.

5. Remove the dish from the fryer basket and allow the cake to cool completely. Spread the buttercream over the cake before serving.

NUTRITION PER 1 SLICE:

TOTAL FAT **14g** • SATURATED FAT **2g** • CHOLESTEROL **0mg** • SODIUM **305mg** • CARBS **46g**
DIETARY FIBERS **1g** • SUGARS **40g** • PROTEIN **1g**

Carrot Cake
with Vanilla Glaze

This treat is a family favorite—a mandatory birthday cake for my husband. It's incredibly moist and filled with carrots, flaxseed, and applesauce.

MAKES **6 slices** • SERVING SIZE **1 slice**

249 CALORIES PER SERVING

FRYER TEMP **310°F**

PREP TIME **10 mins**

COOK TIME **30 mins**

1 tbsp ground flaxseed

3 tbsp water

½ cup cake flour

¼ tsp baking soda

pinch of kosher salt

½ tsp ground cinnamon

½ cup granulated sugar

¼ cup canola oil

½ tsp pure vanilla extract

¼ cup unsweetened applesauce

¾ cup grated carrots

2 tbsp raisins

2 tbsp chopped walnuts

FOR THE GLAZE

⅓ cup powdered sugar

½ tsp pure vanilla extract

2 tsp dairy-free milk (soy recommended)

1. Set the air fryer temp to 310°F. Spray a bundt pan with nonstick cooking spray. Set aside.

2. In a small bowl, combine the flaxseed and water. Set aside for at least 5 minutes.

3. In a large bowl, whisk together the cake flour, baking soda, salt, and cinnamon. Add the sugar, canola oil, vanilla extract, applesauce, and flaxseed mixture. Mix well. Fold in the carrots, raisins, and walnuts. Place the batter in the pan.

4. Place the pan in the fryer basket and bake until a toothpick comes out clean from the center, about 25 to 30 minutes. Turn off the air fryer and allow the pan to sit in the air fryer for 5 minutes.

5. Transfer the cake to a serving platter and allow to cool completely.

6. In a small bowl, make the glaze by whisking together the ingredients. Drizzle the glaze over the cake and allow to set.

7. Cut the cake into 6 slices before serving.

TIP | This recipe also works well with grated zucchini.

TIP | To rapidly set the glaze, freeze the cake for 10 minutes.

NUTRITION PER 1 SLICE:

TOTAL FAT **11g** • SATURATED FAT **1g** • CHOLESTEROL **0mg** • SODIUM **85mg** • CARBS **37g**
DIETARY FIBERS **1g** • SUGARS **27g** • PROTEIN **2g**

Apple Pies

Enjoy these scrumptious pockets of freshly baked apples and toasty cinnamon or make them with any seasonal fruit, such as pears, berries, or peaches.

220 CALORIES PER SERVING

FRYER TEMP **350°F**

PREP TIME **10 mins**

COOK TIME **10 mins**

MAKES **4** • SERVING SIZE **1**

1 medium apple (Gala or Granny Smith recommended), peeled and finely diced

juice of ½ orange

2 tbsp granulated sugar

½ tsp ground cinnamon

2 tsp cornstarch

10oz (285g) vegan pie dough

all-purpose flour

1. Set the air fryer temp to 350°F.

2. In a large bowl, combine the apple, orange juice, sugar, cinnamon, and cornstarch. Mix well.

3. Roll out the dough on a lightly floured surface. Cut the dough into 4 rounds. Place 2 tablespoons of the apple mixture in the center of each. Fold the dough in half and seal the edges with a fork. Make a small slit in the top for steam to escape.

4. Place the pies in the fryer basket and cook until golden brown, about 10 minutes. Turn off the air fryer and allow the pies to cool in the fryer basket for 2 to 3 minutes.

5. Transfer the pies to a wire rack to cool before serving.

TIP | To make homemade dough, in a blender, combine 2 cups of unbleached all-purpose flour, 1 teaspoon of kosher salt, and ½ cup of canola oil in a food processor. Add 5 to 8 tablespoons of cold water and blend until a loose dough forms.

NUTRITION PER 1 PIE:

TOTAL FAT **10g** · SATURATED FAT **1g** · CHOLESTEROL **0mg** · SODIUM **205mg** · CARBS **31g**
DIETARY FIBERS **2g** · SUGARS **13g** · PROTEIN **2g**

Stuffed Apples

You won't need added sugar in this recipe—the apple takes care of all the sweetness. Serve slightly warm with a scoop of dairy-free ice cream.

135 CALORIES PER SERVING

FRYER TEMP **350°F**

PREP TIME **10 mins**

COOK TIME **20 mins**

MAKES **4 servings** • SERVING SIZE **1 serving**

2 small red or green apples, halved horizontally

4 tsp vegan butter (Earth Balance recommended)

¼ tsp ground cardamom

2 tsp ground cinnamon

¼ cup chopped walnuts

¼ cup raisins

pinch of kosher salt

1. Set the air fryer temp to 350°F.

2. Remove the seeds and core from both halves of each apple and place all 4 halves cut side up in a baking dish. Pour about 1 inch (2.5cm) of water into the bottom of the dish.

3. In a medium bowl, combine the butter, cardamom, cinnamon, walnuts, raisins, and salt. Mix well. Equally divide the filling among the apple halves.

4. Place the dish in the fryer basket and bake until the apples are tender, about 20 minutes.

5. Remove the dish from the fryer basket and allow the apples to cool for 10 minutes before serving.

TIP | For larger apples, add 5 minutes to the cooking time.

NUTRITION PER 1 SERVING:

TOTAL FAT **6g** • SATURATED FAT **0g** • CHOLESTEROL **0mg** • SODIUM **209mg** • CARBS **20g**
DIETARY FIBERS **4g** • SUGARS **14g** • PROTEIN **2g**

Raspberry & Pineapple Sundaes

366 CALORIES PER SERVING

FRYER TEMP **400°F**

PREP TIME **10 mins**

COOK TIME **5 mins**

Adding a brûléed crust to sweet, juicy pineapple makes this dessert extra special. Top the sundae with homemade agave and pistachio granola.

MAKES **4** • SERVING SIZE **1**

2 cups diced pineapple

½ tsp ground cinnamon

½ tsp granulated sugar

1 cup raspberries

¾ cup dairy-free ice cream

½ cup **Agave & Pistachio Granola** (pg. 38)

1. Set the air fryer temp to 400°F. Spray the fryer basket with nonstick cooking spray.

2. In a medium bowl, combine the pineapple, cinnamon, and sugar. Toss well to coat.

3. Place the pineapple in the fryer basket and cook until sizzling and the sugar begins to caramelize, about 5 minutes.

4. Remove the pineapple from the fryer basket and allow to cool slightly. Serve the pineapple over the ice cream. Top each sundae with an equal amount of Agave & Pistachio Granola and raspberries.

TIP | Swap dairy-free yogurt for the ice cream and enjoy this for breakfast.

TIP | For easier cleanup, place the pineapple in a baking dish.

NUTRITION PER 1 SUNDAE:

TOTAL FAT **14g** • SATURATED FAT **2g** • CHOLESTEROL **0mg** • SODIUM **187mg** • CARBS **58g** DIETARY FIBERS **5g** • SUGARS **38g** • PROTEIN **3g**

Chocolate Chip Cookie Cups

This decadent treat is perfectly portioned. Easily make this recipe gluten-free by replacing the flour with the same amount of gluten-free baking mix.

MAKES **4** • SERVING SIZE **1**

291 CALORIES PER SERVING

FRYER TEMP **340°F**

PREP TIME **10 mins**

COOK TIME **10 mins**

1 tbsp ground flaxseed

3 tbsp water

1 cup all-purpose flour

½ tsp baking powder

¼ tsp kosher salt

3 tbsp maple syrup

2 tbsp coconut oil, melted

¼ cup vegan chocolate chips

1. Set the air fryer temp to 340°F. Spray 4 ramekins with nonstick cooking spray. Set aside.

2. In a small bowl, combine the flaxseed and water.

3. In a medium bowl, whisk together the flour, baking powder, and salt. Add the flaxseed mixture, maple syrup, and coconut oil. Mix until just combined. Fold in the chocolate chips. Place an equal amount of batter into each ramekin.

4. Place the ramekins in the fryer basket and bake until puffed and slightly golden, about 8 to 10 minutes.

5. Remove the ramekins from the fryer basket and allow the cookie cups to cool slightly before serving.

TIP | Bake these ahead of time and reheat for 2 minutes in the air fryer.

TIP | If you're a fan of raw cookie dough, reduce the cook time to 7 to 8 minutes to up the gooey factor.

NUTRITION PER 1 CUP:

TOTAL FAT **12g** • SATURATED FAT **8g** • CHOLESTEROL **0mg** • SODIUM **150mg** • CARBS **45g**
DIETARY FIBERS **1g** • SUGARS **9g** • PROTEIN **5g**

Chocolate, Orange & Chia Pudding Tarts

These tarts need many steps, but they're worth them. Chia seeds have omega-3 fats, which help promote a healthy heart, neurological system, skin, and eyes.

270 CALORIES PER SERVING

FRYER TEMP **350°F**

PREP TIME **20 mins**

COOK TIME **10 mins**

MAKES **6** • SERVING SIZE **1**

1 cup chocolate soy milk

¼ cup chia seeds

1 tbsp orange zest

pinch of sea salt

2 cups all-purpose flour

½ tsp kosher salt

½ cup canola oil

5 to 8 tbsp cold water

1. In a 16-ounce (475-milliliter) glass jar, whisk together the soy milk, chia seeds, orange zest, and sea salt. Allow the mixture to sit for 10 minutes before whisking again. Cover and refrigerate for at least 6 hours. (If you don't have a whisk that fits inside the glass jar, you can use a medium bowl to whisk together the ingredients.)

2. Set the air fryer temp to 350°F.

3. In a medium bowl, combine the flour and kosher salt.

4. In a separate medium bowl, combine the oil and 5 to 6 tablespoons of the water. Make a well in the center of the flour mixture and pour in the oil mixture. Mix with a fork until just combined. Add 1 to 2 more tablespoons of water as needed. Shape the dough into a ball.

5. Roll out the dough between 2 sheets of wax or parchment paper. Use a 4.5-inch (11.5cm) ring mold to cut out 6 rounds. Transfer the dough to ramekins and press in gently to form the cups.

6. Place the ramekins in the fryer basket and bake until the crust is golden, about 10 minutes.

7. Remove the ramekins from the fryer basket and allow the cups to cool completely. Transfer the cups to a platter. Fill the cups with the chia pudding and serve immediately.

TIP | You can make the chia pudding up to 3 days in advance.

NUTRITION PER 1 TART:

TOTAL FAT **12g** • SATURATED FAT **1g** • CHOLESTEROL **0mg** • SODIUM **217mg** • CARBS **31g**
DIETARY FIBERS **4g** • SUGARS **3g** • PROTEIN **6g**

Index

Acknowledgments

This book is for all those veggie skeptics out there. I know food can't be good for you without tasting amazing. These recipes are stellar examples of how delicious plant-based foods are.

A shout-out to my local Connecticut farmers, especially the Gazy family, who deliver a CSA (community-supported agriculture) box to my door almost every week year-round.

I'm tremendously proud to put out another title with DK Publishing. Christopher Stolle and his team of designers and recipe testers are simply the best, and I'm incredibly grateful for their expertise and guidance. And finally, to my family, who's always willing to try new things—and give me their *brutally* honest opinions. They make me a better chef every day.

Publisher's Acknowledgments

The publisher would like to thank Ashley Brooks for preparing the food at the photo shoot and Savannah Norris for food styling. The publisher would also like to thank Irena Kutza and Lexi Winder for testing the recipes. We couldn't have created this book without all of you!

Dana Angelo White (MS, RD, ATC) is a registered dietitian, certified athletic trainer, and nutrition and fitness consultant. She's the nutrition expert for Food Network.com and the founding contributor for Food Network's Healthy Eats blog.

Dana is the sports dietitian and assistant clinical faculty in the Department of Athletic Training and Sports Medicine at Quinnipiac University in Hamden, Connecticut. She resides in Fairfield, Connecticut, with her husband, three children, and Boston Terrier, Violet Pickles.